LEAVE STORY FOR TORTOISE

Mustapha Anako

authorHOUSE

AuthorHouse™
1663 Liberty Drive
Bloomington, IN 47403
www.authorhouse.com
Phone: 833-262-8899

Published by AuthorHouse 03/17/2022

ISBN: 978-1-6655-5492-3 (sc)
ISBN: 978-1-6655-5493-0 (hc)
ISBN: 978-1-6655-5494-7 (e)

Library of Congress Control Number: 2022905031

To my mom and dad, Ret. MWO Lawal SiakaYusufu and Saratu Anako, for their support during my struggle

To Dr Jibril Odogba and Susie Odogba for providing during very tough times for the entire family.

To my wife, Ahuoiza Ohunene Anako, whom I simply call Nene, for her support during her own struggle.

To Marc Inda-Enesi and Rachael Ize-Ometere, my blessings from above.

To Fatima Yusuf, may your soul continue to rest well.

To Enezi Lawal, it still hurts not to know what happened to you.

CONTENTS

PREFACE

The plight of the average Nigerian inspired me to write this book. The tears, the pain, the blood, and the sorrow the average Nigerian must endure for being a Nigerian is mind-boggling. In life, there will be pain caused by unfortunate incidents, such as being sick and succumbing to that sickness. In Nigeria, the pain, tears, and sorrow the people face are often man-made.

Most times, when you hear a Nigerian died of a road accident, you will discover it was caused by potholes on roads. A pothole that was left unfixed by a government that did not live up to one of its responsibilities of fixing bad roads. An illegal checkpoint by the police or an armed law enforcement officer sometimes leads to deadly accidents in the highways. Armed bandits are also responsible for fatal road accidents. As a result of these senseless accidents, families lose breadwinners, and the country loses great minds. In Nigeria, you often hear sad stories of students who just finished their final exams from college or university and died in a road accident on their way home.

Nigerians have lost their lives due to the prevalence of fake drugs in the country. This makes one wonder if there is a functional government responsible for ensuring Nigerians are safe from these drugs you find in legitimate pharmacies. Many Nigerian citizens have lost their lives simply waiting for medical service in various hospitals and clinics.

Many brothers and sisters have died at the hands of law enforcement officers, who think they have the ultimate right to beat you up and even shoot to kill you—with no consequence. These same law enforcement officers can run you over on the road with their vehicles, sometimes while driving in the wrong lane or going in the opposite direction of the flow of traffic—again with absolutely no lawful consequence for their actions.

In Nigeria, one's experience of government institutions leaves one feeling that these institutions are run and executed to cause pain and hardship while undertaking simple processes like getting a driver's license, state identification, passport, or approval documents for various tasks. The government cannot create jobs; neither has it been able to build and nurture thriving economic grounds that would enable average citizens to easily set up businesses and create their own jobs.

Amid Nigeria's pain and dysfunction, Nigerians are unique people. They are resilient; even when all might seem dim and gloomy, Nigerians do not give up easily. As they say in Nigeria, "Nigerians no dey carry last" (You will not find a Nigerian being last in any endeavour).

ACKNOWLEDGEMENTS

Thanks to Goodman Shodeinde (aka Baba G), for taking the time to look through my writing despite your tight schedule.

Fist in the air for Dr Jibril Odogba, aka G. Papa, for editing and helping with resources to publish a book. You are, indeed, the elder of the family. All those family trips you sponsored also led to the inspiration for writing this book.

Akira to Andy N. Ajiduah for the design of the cover of the book.

As they say on the streets of Nigeria, "'Nough respect" to Dr Poundo (Poundedyamcious Emeritus 1) for his poundedyamcious insight. I have always desired a Nigerian to help me with my book. And the Almighty Creator used social media to bring you to me to aid me in finishing this book. Twenty gbosa for you!

INTRODUCTION

Nigeria is the birthplace of African achievers. It is the most populous black nation in the world. The citizens of the country are some of the most creative people one will come across. Nigerians are very adaptive to any situation they find themselves in. Despite all the challenges the average Nigerian faces, they work daily to thrive in a country where things seem to be going in the opposite direction. Nigerians always have a way of circumventing every challenging situation they come across, and they're exceptionally good at coming up with words or expressions to survive a difficult situation. Despite many languages or dialects spoken in Nigeria and the national lingua franca being English, Nigerians have been able to unify under the language popularly called "Pidgin English" also known as "broken" English. While the origins of certain words and phrases in Pidgin English will never be known, one part of the country, Warri in Delta State, Nigeria, will be credited for introducing certain words and phrases in Pidgin English. Thorough appreciation of the words, proverbs, and idiomatic expressions in Pidgin English spoken by Nigerians requires an understanding of Pidgin English and of Nigerians as a people, their struggles and challenges, and their history. For instance, where did the word "katakata" comes from? While I want to believe the globally acclaimed Nigerian Afrobeat king (Fela) made the word popular in the Pidgin English vocabulary, the word is likely from one of over 800 languages spoken in Nigeria.

When a Nigerian says, "Yawa don gas," it means "All hell has broken loose." Despite being a unifying and organically developed Nigerian language, Nigerian Pidgin English still has some expressions and statements not fully understood by every Nigerian, due to the initial resistance by some Nigerians to adopt the language. For example, to an average Nigerian, the assertion, "The thing tear shirt!" literally translates to, "Something tore a shirt!" However, "The thing tear shirt!" means "It is expensive!"

Nigerians are incredibly special people; there is something unique in every tribe, and there is vast diversity in culture and language. In most parts, Nigerians are brothers and sisters united by the land they call their land of origin, Nigeria, irrespective of the history that led to such unification. Despite Nigeria's abundance of natural resources, the average Nigerian is not living life to the fullest.

In the Nigerian national anthem, a line reads, "The labour of our heroes past shall never be in vain."[1] Most of its heroes in various disciplines or walks of life have been long forgotten, even though some Nigerians have excelled both at home and on the global stage. In Nigeria, there are no proper records of the works of both its citizens and those whose origins began in Nigeria. Either the audio, visual, and written records of their heroes past are missing, or co-ordinated efforts to curate them correctly were not executed. These reasons are, in part, why I wrote this book on Pidgin English, for I believe our heroes past left Nigerians with a foundational treasure that truly unifies them— Nigerian Pidgin English. For clarity, heroes define every Nigerian, past or present, who had the courage (either consciously or unconsciously) to embrace and develop Pidgin English as a unification language for Nigerians.

---

[1] Nigeria Galleria, "The National Anthem," https://www.nigeriagalleria.com/Nigeria/National-Anthems-Pledge.html.

It's easy to give up hope, it's easy to be depressed, and it's understandable to call it quits in Nigeria. It's a country where the law enforcement officers (who are also Nigerians) treat you like black South Africans were once treated in the old apartheid system in South Africa by their law enforcement officers.

In Nigeria, the citizens are not guaranteed a constant power supply despite the wealth of the country. In a country where politicians earn more than their counterparts in advanced countries, it is understandable why some Nigerians might want to call it quits. But then, when you dig beyond the surface of what is popularly advertised and discover the deep potentials of Nigerians, their history, food, cultures, and traditions, as embodied within Nigerian Pidgin English, you will also understand why Nigeria is a country one will want to see bloom to its full potentials.

As the saying goes, there is power in "the Word", requiring people to have faith. Nigerians are people of faith. Nigeria is the only country where you will find three different churches in the same building, along with a mosque or two on the same street. and in some places, there could be five or more churches, along with mosques and shrines on the same street. The people are religious and fetish all at the same time. There is so much religion in the land; and yet, Nigeria buckles at the knees with heaps of wrong deeds that will make you wonder what life would be like if the people didn't have religion. Simply put, Nigeria is a special place, and the people are exceptional.

To grasp and understand a language—as well as the correct context in which certain words, phrases, sentences, and statements are best used—and to correctly communicate in that language requires a journey through the complexities of the language. The complexities of a language are better understood when one gains a deeper understanding of the people who speak it, their collective history, and the daily challenges they face that has led to the development of such a language.

The phrase "leave story for tortoise" connotes a very curious saying by Nigerian elders. The tortoise is known to be very slow. but in its slowness, it is able to see the world as it is, gathering the stories of the world around it. And based on its long-life span, the tortoise is an elder who is a walking library of stories (at the end of it all, each of us is here to create and live out our own unique story or a unique collective story with others). Its library of stories can provide one with wisdom and a guide one to living in, surviving, and navigating this challenging world.

The above trait is inherent within Pidgin English words, phrases, and sentences/statements. Each Pidgin English word, phrase, or sentence/statement, encapsulates a unique story that cuts across the various cultures in the land of origin, Nigeria, where these phrases were developed and used for communication.

You will find the journey through this book has three distinct parts. In "Part 1: Nigerian Pidgin English Words and Their Meanings," you'll find a quick glossary of Pidgin English words, their meanings and usage, organised to quickly get you up and running. "Part 2: Nigeria and Nigerians" explores Nigeria as a country and its people who created this language to enable themselves to communicate in a unique way that encapsulates their history and stories. In "Part 3: 100 Common Pidgin English Expressions with Wisdom" you'll find words of wisdom in Pidgin English used by Nigerian people to safeguard, nurture, and evolve their communities, cultures, and way of life.

I have organised the book thusly to enable you to traverse the journey through *Leave Story for Tortoise* along the best path that suits you. And I hope that you enjoy your journey through it.

PART I

NIGERIAN PIDGIN ENGLISH WORDS AND THEIR MEANINGS

CHAPTER 1

ACTION TIME NA GHEN GHEN!

The case can be made that Nigerian Pidgin English is the unofficial national language of Nigeria. Pidgin English is what unifies every Nigerian. Pidgin English—also known as "broken" or simply "pidgin"—is the most comfortable way to communicate in Nigeria if you do not want to be made fun of because you cannot speak the Queen's English.

Nigerian Pidgin English (NPE) has a large vocabulary. Even today, it is an evolving language, with words constantly added in daily conversational use. I will focus on defining and explaining the most common words. While most Nigerians do not know the origins of these words, some are believed to have been adopted from the many dialects spoken in Nigeria. It is critical to know that certain words may have different connotations, and some have different spellings, depending on their pronunciation.

After I look into how these words are constructed and used, I will discuss them in the context of communicating, particularly in the expression of wisdom in the form of a proverb or a parable. Some of the words in this chapter will be found in the hundred statements compiled in part III of this book, "100 Common Pidgin English Expressions with Wisdom."

A

agbero (*ah-bay-row*), NOUN: a tout, often found in a motor park, airport, or busy commercial area
The guy na agbero. (The guy is a tout.)
NPE synonym: *area-boy*

argro (*ah-grow*), NOUN: sexual urge, horniness
As I see that girl nyash inside that jeans wey she wear, argro begin catch me (With the sight of the girl's butt inside her jeans, horniness overcame me [the sight of the girl's butt inside her jeans made me feel horny]).

ajebutter (*ah-jeer-butter*), NOUN: (1) a person with a privileged upbringing (2) a person who has not experienced hardship in life

This ajebutter no know how to wash plate. (This person who has had an easy life does not know how to do the dishes.)

akamu (*ah-car-mu*), NOUN: pap made from corn

Na only akamu I take today. (I have had only pap all day.)

NPE synonym: *ogi*

akara (*ah-car-ra*), NOUN: (1) bean bun made from beans that have been mashed and fried

The akara sweet well well. (The bean bun is extremely sweet.)

(2) something easy

To be doctor no be akara. (Becoming a doctor is not an easy thing.)

amebo (*ah-me-bor*), NOUN: a rumour peddler

VERB: gossip

You like to dey do amebo. (You like to gossip.)

awoof (*ah-woof*), noun: (1) a freebie or free stuff (2) an underserved gain

Awoof dey run belle. (Free stuff will upset your stomach.)

B

bakassi (*bar-car-see*), NOUN: (1) a big buttock, usually in reference to a woman's behind

The woman get big bakassi. (The woman has a big behind.)

NPE synonyms: *nyash* or *nyansh*

(2) PROPER NOUN: Bakassi, a peninsula on the Gulf of Guinea between Cameroon and Nigeria that is a place of dispute between the two countries

baff (*baf*), NOUN: (1) to shower (2) to take a bath
I nova/never baff today. (I have not taken a bath today.)

baffs (*bafs*), NOUN: (1) new cloth or new clothes.
This your baffs correct! (Your new dress/clothes is/are fine.)

biabia (*beer-beer*), NOUN: beards
You need to cut your biabia. (You need to shave your beard).
The word "cut" is normally used.

blocus or blocos (*blur-cos*), NOUN: a man's testicles

> *The man get big blocus.* (The man has big testicles. Or, as the Americans say, the man has big balls.)

blalar (*bla-lar*), NOUN/VERB: (1) To whip or whop (2) To beat up

> *Student wey no listen, go get blalar.* (A student who does not listen will get a whooping or get beaten.)
> NPE: *koboko*

C

canda (*can-dar*), NOUN: (1) tough leather skin (2) foreskin

> *I beg, put canda for my rice.* (Please add tough meat to my rice.)

chop (*chop*), VERB: (1) to eat (2) to have sex

> *I go chop rice.* (I will eat rice.)

> *I chop the babe.* (I had sex with the woman.)

> *I chop the guy.* (I had sex with the man.)

> NPE synonym: *wack*

chop-up (*chop-up*), VERB: (1) to enlarge (2) to become bigger

> *I really need to chop-up.* (I really need to become bigger.)

comot or **komot** (*core-moth*), VERB: (1) to get out (2) to move (3) to remove

(1) *I comot the chair from my house.* (I removed the chair from my house.)

(2) *Abeg, comot from my room.* (Please get out of my room.)

D

dey(*day*), VERB: (1) is (2) am

I dey here. (I am here.)

Why dey here? (Who is there?)

dabaru (*da-bar-ru*), VERB: (1) scatter (2) destroy

I go dabaru the game. (I will scatter/destroy the game.)

dundee (*don-dee*), NOUN/ADJECTIVE: (1) dumb (2) stupid (3) fool

I am sorry to say, you be dundee! (I am sorry to say it, you are a dummy!)

NPE synonym: *mumu*

E

efico or **efiko** (*e-fee-co*) NOUN, (1) bookworm (2) brilliant person

The girl/ boy na efico. (The girl/boy is a bookworm.)

efisi (*e-fee-see*) NOUN, (1) style (2) charisma

> *Enough efisi.* (Enough style.)

> *The man/woman get efisi.* (The man/woman has charisma.)

egunje (*eg-goon-je*) NOUN/VERB, bribe

> *The police say make I give am egunje before I fit pass.* (The police demanded I give him a bribe before I could pass.)

> NPE synonym: *settle*

F

fabu (*far-boo*) NOUN, (1) made-up story (2) fabrication (3) fiction

> *Your confession na fabu.* (Your confession is all a fabrication.)

> NPE synonym: *lie*

faji (*far-gee*) NOUN, (1) pleasure (2) enjoyment

> *Na faji we dey so!* (We are enjoying!)

flenjor (*flen-jor*) VERB, enjoy

> *I see you and your babe dey flenjor.* (I see you and your babe enjoying.)

> NPE synonym: *faji*

G

gbedu (*gbe-do*) NOUN, (1) music (2) party

> *The gbedu wey 2face release na correct gbedu.* (The music that 2face released is good music.)

gbosa (*bow-sar*) noun, (1) alarming sound (2) sudden sound

> *Na sleep I dey when I just hear gbosa!* (I was sleeping when I suddenly heard a loud sound!)

gorimapa (*go-re-ma-pa*) ADJECTIVE/NOUN, (1) a head without any hair (2) completely bald (3) a person with no hair on their head

> *Call gorimapa for me.* (Call that person without hair for me.)

graga (*gra-gra*) NOUN, aggression

> Your gragra too much; you need to cool down. (Your aggression is too much; you need to slow down.)

H

hammer (*ha-ma*) NOUN/VERB, (1) to hit a jackpot (2) suddenly making it big time (3) to have sex.

> *I don hammer!* (I have made it big time!)

> *I hammer the babe.* (I had sex with the woman.)

> NPE synonym: *nack*

I

igebo (*eg-bow*) NOUN, marijuana

> *You dey behave like person wey smoke igebo.* (You are acting like you smoked marijuana.)

> NPE synonym: *gbana*

ikebe (*e-kay-bay*) NOUN, (1) buttock, often a big buttock

> *The woman ikeba, no be joke!* (The woman's buttock is no joke.)

> NPE synonyms: *nyash* or *nyansh*

iyawo (*e-yah-wooh*) NOUN, (1) new wife (2) wife
Na my iyawo be that. (That is my wife.)

J

jagajaga (*jar-gar-jar-gar*) ADJECTIVE, (1) messy (2) unarranged

> *My room dey jagajaga, right now.* (My room is messy/unarranged right now.)

> NPE synonym: *nyamanyama*

jazz (*jazz*) NOUN/VERB, (1) voodoo (2) to bewitch (3) nonsense

> *The wife dey use jazz control the husband.* (The wife is using voodoo to control the husband.)

> *All that talk na jazz.* (All that talk is nonsense.)

jeje (*jeer-jeer*) ADJECTIVE, (1) easy (2) gentle

> *Me? I dey jeje.* (Me? I am gentle/easy.)

JJC (*jay-jay-see*) NOUN, (1) a novice (2) a newcomer (3) a first-timer

> The term was made popular by Fela Anikulapo Kuti in one of his songs, "JJC (Johnny Just Come)".
>
> *When e come to woman matter, the boy na JJC.* (When it comes to the issues of women, the boy is a novice.)

juju (*juju*) NOUN/VERB, (1) voodoo (2) bewitch (3) charm or a portion of charm (4) a brand of music in the Yoruba tribe

> *You put juju for mouth follow me talk?* (Did you put charm or voodoo in your mouth to talk to me?)
>
> NPE synonym; *jazz*

K

kaikai (*ky-ky*) NOUN, (1) local gin

> *I need to drink kaikai to fit sleep well.* (I need to drink gin to sleep well)

kolo (*kolo*) VERB, (1) to go crazy (2) to go mad (3) to have a mental breakdown

> *The guy don kolo.* (The guy has gone mad.)

kampe (*cam-pay*) ADJECTIVE, (1) strong (2) solid (3) unshakeable (4) okay

The table dey kampe! (The table is solid!)

I dey kampe! (I am unshakeable!)

kasala (*car-sa-lar*) NOUN, trouble

The man don enter heavy kasala. (The man is in big trouble.)

NPE synonyms: *wahala, palava*

kata (*car-tar*) NOUN, mucus from the nose

Abeg, blow the kata from your nose. (Please, blow the mucus from your nose.)

katakata (*car-tar-car-tar*) NOUN, (1) chaos (2) trouble

If you no pay me my money, katakata go burst. (If you do not pay me my money, there will be trouble.)

NPE synonyms: *kasala, yawa, palavar*

koboko (*co-bow-co*) NOUN/VERB, (1) horsewhip (2) whip (3) cane

The pikin chop koboko because e steal meat from pot. (The child got whipped because he stole meat from the pot.)

NPE synonyms: *blala* (a word from the Hausa language of the Hausa tribe of Nigeria)

kolo (*co-lo*) NOUN/ADJECTIVE, (1) insane (2) gone made

> *The man don kolo finish.* (The man has gone completely mad.)

kurukere (*coo-ru-ke-re*) ADJECTIVE, (1) dubious (2) shady

> *I see say your movement dey kurekere.* (I see that your movement is dubious.)

M

magomago (*mar-go-mar-go*) NOUN, (1) trick (2) shady

> *You wan do me magomago.* (You want to trick me.)

> NPE synonym: *wayo*

mugu (*moo-goo*) ADJECTIVE, (1) dumb (2) an idiot

> *The guy/babe na mugu.* (The man/woman is dumb.)

> *Na mugu you be?* (Are you an idiot?)

> NPE synonym: *mumu*

mumsi (*mum-see*) NOUN, (1) mother

> *Dey say I look like my mumsi.* (They say I look like my mother.)

mumu (*moo-moo*) NOUN, (1) a fool (2) an idiot

> *The guy/babe na mumu.* (The man/woman is a fool.)

> *Na mumu you be?* (Are you an idiot?)

> NPE synonym: *mugu*

N

nack (*nack*) VERB, (1) hit (2) sex

> *The policeman nack me for head.* (The policeman hit me on the head.)

> *I go like to nack that fine woman.* (I would like to have sex with that beautiful woman.)

> *I go like to nack that fine man.* (I would like to have sex with that handsome man.)

nyamanyama (nya-mar-nya-mar) ADJECTIVE, (1) rotten (2) messy

> *I no fit eat nyamanyama food.* (I can't eat rotten food.)

> NPE synonym: *jagajaga*

nyash or **nyansh** (*nyash* or *nyansh*) NOUN, buttock

> *The pikin nyash dirty.* (The baby's buttock is dirty.)

> NPE synonym: *bakasi*

O

ojoro (*oh-joe-row*) NOUN/ADJECTIVE, (1) cheat (2) trickery

>   *Abeg, no do me ojoro.* (Please, do not cheat me.)

>   NPE synonym: *wayo*

olodo (*oh-low-dough*) NOUN/ADJECTIVE, (1) a daft (2) a dummy

>   *I no expect am to pass the exam; the boy na olodo.* (I do not expect him to pass the exam; the boy is a dummy.)

>   NPE synonyms: *dundee, mumu*

oyinbo (*oh-yeen-booh*) NOUN, a Caucasian

>   Oyinbo man dey my house. (A Caucasian man is in my house.)

oga (*or- gar*) noun, (1) a boss (2) the head

>   *My oga!* (My boss!)

>   *My wife, na oga of the house.* (My wife is the boss of the house.)

P

paddy or **padi** (*par-dee*) NOUN, friend

>   *The guy na my paddy.* (The guy is my friend.)

palavar (par-la-var) NOUN, trouble

> *Leave me alone if you no want palavar.* (Leave me alone if you do not want trouble.)

> NPE synonym: *wahala, kasala*

pam (*pam*) VERB, (1) chill out

> *When I see police, I pam.* (When I saw the police, I chilled out).

pepper (*pepper*) NOUN, (1) money (2) trouble

> *My guy, pepper no rest.* (My guy, there is no money.)

> *Talk to me anyhow. I go show you pepper.* (Watch what you say to me. I will give you trouble.)

pikin (*pee-kin*) NOUN, child

> *The pikin dey play.* (The child is playing.)

popsi (*pop-see*) NOUN, (1) father (2) dad

> *My popsi na soldier.* (My dad is a soldier.)

R

runs (*runs*) VERB, (1) activity (2) prostitution

> *The girl dey do runs.* (The girl is a prostitute.)

The babe na runs girl.

Who dey in charge of the runs here? (Who's in charge of the activity here?)

S

shack (*shark*) NOUN/VERB, (1) drink (2) intoxication

I need to shack gari. (I need to drink gari.)

Your love dey shack me. (Your love is getting me intoxicated.)

shakara (*sha-car-ra*) VERB, show-off

It is believed to be from the Yoruba word "shakor".

The guy like to dey do shakara with im car. (The guy likes showing off with his car.)

NPE synonyms: *yanga*

shayo (*sha-yo*) ADJECTIVE/NOUN/VERB, (1) to drink alcohol (2) a drunk (3) drinking alcohol

The guy na shayo. (The guy is a drunk.)

The guy don shayo. (The guy is drunk.)

I dey shayo. (I am drinking alcohol.)

T

toto (*to-to*) NOUN, (1) a local government area in Nasarawa state in Nigeria, not known by many (2) popular and common slang for the vagina

> *The man wan touch my toto.* (The man wants to touch my vagina.)

W

wayo (*wa-yo*) NOUN, trickery

> *Abeg, no do me wayo.* (Please, do not try to trick me)

> NPE synonym: *ojoro*

waka or **wakawaka** (*wah-car* or *wah-car-wah-car*) VERB, walk

> *My waka/wakawaka make me tire.* (My walk made me tired.)

waytin or **wetin** (*way-tin, waiting*) PRONOUN, what

> *Waytin/Wetin happen for here?!* (What happened here?!)

wack (*wack*) VERB, to eat

> *I just wack rice.* (I just ate rice)

> NPE synonym: *chop*

Y

yab (*yab*) VERB, (1) to make fun of (2) to insult someone

> *Dey yab me because I fall for ground.* (They made fun of me because I fell to the ground.)

> *I yab the yeye man.* (I insulted the foolish man.)

yakata (*yah-car-tar*) ADVERB, uncontrollable

> *As I dey go market, I fall yakata for road.* (On my way to the market, I fell to the road uncontrollably.)

yanga (*yan-gah*) ADJECTIVE/VERB, (1) show-off (2) hard to get (3) swag

> *I dey try toast the babe, but she dey do yanga.* (I am trying to toast the babe [ask her out], but she is playing hard to get.)

> *You dey use your new car, do yanga.* (You are showing off with your new car.)

> NPE synonym: *shakara*

yawa (*ya-wa*) NOUN, (1) trouble (2) bad situation

> *I don enter yawa!* (I am in big trouble!)

> NPE synonym: *kasala*

yeye (*yeer-yeer*) ADJECTIVE, foolish

> *The man na yeye man.* (The man is a foolish man)

PART II

NIGERIA AND NIGERIANS

CHAPTER 2

NA WE BE THIS

Certain statements by the elders in Nigeria are viewed as words of wisdom by Nigerians. The elders believe that statements are not just a grouping of words spoken; they provide a guide to surviving this challenging world—and this may be the root of how Pidgin English came to be in Nigeria. Sometimes, these statements made by Nigerian elders are intricate and require an explanation to enable you to comprehend and appreciate the meaning. Or they may be simple facts of life. When someone says, "Na we be this," they are saying, "This is who we are!"

Nigeria is known for many things, but one area people have not fully explored is the Nigerian Pidgin English words Nigerians use in their daily vocabulary. While the documented unifying language in Nigeria is English—or should I say the Queen's English—Nigeria has an organic language that everyone fully understands, and that is Nigerian Pidgin English.

NPE is also known as broken English or, simply, brokin' or pidgin. There are words in NPE that still need to be explained, words whose origins some Nigerians, if not most, don't know. But when these words are used in context, and articulated with facial expressions and body movements, every Nigerian understands the wisdom and messages they convey.

To learn, understand, appreciate, and correctly use words in NPE, it's important to understand the country called Nigeria; Nigerians; and the environment in which Nigerians live, along with their challenges and their triumphs.

Nigeria is a great country in the western part of Africa. It's the most populous black nation in the world. Nigeria is often referred to as the Giant of Africa, not because of the size of the population, but more because of its abundant natural and human resources. If there was ever a picture of a blessed country in the dictionary, it would be a picture of Nigeria.

Nigeria is among the N11 countries—the next eleven emerging economies to look out for in the future. The name was coined by the leading global investment bank known as Goldman Sachs. These N11 countries are Bangladesh, Egypt, Indonesia, Iran, Mexico, Nigeria, Pakistan, the Philippines, South Korea, Turkey, and Vietnam. One of the reasons Nigeria is in this group is its young population—and the purchasing power it will have in the future if the country is able to overcome its challenges. Nigeria sure has a lot of challenges.

Nigeria (also called Naija "9jah" by Nigerian youths) is such a unique place one can only appreciate it by having lived in and had the opportunity to travel intensively around the country. Interacting with the people in various parts of the country enables one to understand why Nigeria is such a special place.

Various sources on Nigeria state that Nigeria has three major languages, despite the fact that over 300 languages are spoken in the country. If there was ever a city of Babel in the present world, it would be Nigeria. Despite the different languages, the various ethnic backgrounds, and the various religious beliefs, Nigerians strive to live together as one people. Nigerians marry outside their ethnic backgrounds, and their different religious backgrounds have not stopped them from uniting either. Intertribal marriages are common among the people in the western and eastern parts of the country, which comprises the Yoruba tribe in the west and the Ibo tribe to the east.

Despite the integration of people in Nigeria, occasional violence caused by ethnic and religious beliefs rears its ugly head every now and then.

Nevertheless, in most parts, Nigerians live in peace with each other. There is an almost even distribution of the population among the two major world religions (Christianity and Islam). There are also many people in Nigeria who practise and professing other local religious beliefs. And some Nigerians combine practising their local religions with being either a Christian or a Muslim. Often you will find people from the same family all individually practising their chosen religion and living in peace. Polygamy is not a crime, so it is not strange to see a man married to more than one woman in Nigeria.

Despite the blessings from above, most Nigerians are suffering amid plenty. Irrespective of their status, location, and position in life, most Nigerians are passionate about Nigeria. Nigerians will tell you that the only disasters in the country are the leaders and politicians, who have had the opportunity to transform Nigeria into a paradise but have lacked the vision to move the country to the twenty-first century. Nigerian political leaders are worse than any known natural disaster because of their lack of vision and leadership skills. It is said that, to whom much is given, much is expected in return. The political class has had a whole lot given to them. The question most Nigerians ask themselves is, How have our leaders made life better for the average citizen?

Most Nigerians, even those in the diaspora, cannot help but talk about Nigeria's challenges. When Nigerians in diaspora meet at a party or any social functions, the problems and situations in Nigeria dominate their conversations. People often joke that the only bad thing about Nigeria is that it is filled with Nigerians. Love it or hate it, Nigeria is always on the mind of every Nigerian, no matter their location or status.

One thing you can give to the average Nigerian is their sense of style when it comes to fashion. You will often hear people say that fashion is in Paris. That's because they've never been to Nigeria. In Nigeria, image is everything, and looking good is good business. Thanks to *Black Panther*, the movie by Marvel Comics, Nigerians have come to appreciate their local style of fashion once again. It often takes the Western countries to repackage Africa's ideas before people in Africa take note.

A fashion statement in Nigeria is not just about style; it also has to do with dignity. Your neighbour should not look down on you; you do not want people being condescending to you just because of your looks. Nigerians are people with pride and dignity. One of the ways Nigerians hide their poverty is the way they dress. If you are not well off, you do not want the community to make fun of or look down of you.

There is one thing constant in the traditional fashion styles in Nigeria for men across the country—a special cap or hat over the head. The men in the eastern part of the country are known to wear a colourful cap, made popular by a character called Okoro in a TV show called *The Village Headmaster*. Sometimes there is a long feather in the cap. Having a feather in your cap is a way to distinguish between who is and is not considered a chief. Wearing a red hat is also a way to distinguish whether you're worthy to be called a chief. The men in the delta region of Nigeria wear bowler hats, which often go with a white shirt and a wrapper tied around their waists. This style of dressing comes with no visible socks in their shoes. In the western part of the country, the top of their outfit is it simply called *buba*, the pants are *shokoto*, and their popular hats are called *fila*. There is a special fabric called *asho-oke* that's worn on special occasions. There is a special triangular-looking hat (when viewed from the side), which is also worn by the brothers in the west. Men from the northern part of Nigeria have a style made from kaftan. Babanriga or agbada is a style common to men in the north and western parts of the country. Over the years, as the people have integrated, so have styles crossed over to different parts of the country.

When it comes to the style women wear in Nigeria, words alone do not suffice. Starting with their headgear, popularly known as *gele*, women's fashion in Nigeria is out of this world.

It is usually tricky for a man to describe a female outfit; in Nigeria, this is no exception. Women's fashion in Nigeria is all about elegance. The styles are sophisticated. To describe them wouldn't do justice to what Nigerian women wear. The Marvel Studios movie *Black Panther* gives you an insight into what Nigerian women look like in their local attire. The recent movie by Eddie Murphy (*Coming 2 America*) will also give you an insight into the various styles of Nigerian women's fashion.

The headgear is usually a sight to look forward to. Take the one Gladys Knight wore when she performed a song called "Midnight Train to Zamunda" for the king of the fictitious nation of Zamunda in *Coming 2 Africa*. While various tribes have different names for the headgear, its popular name, gele, comes from the Yoruba tribe in the western part of Nigeria. A word of wisdom: At all times, be sure not to sit behind a

25

woman wearing gele in a movie theatre, in church, or on any occasion where you want to have a great view of what is in front of you. Some gele are so high the sunroof of a car has to be opened to accommodate them when a Nigerian woman is heading out to an event.

One of the things that makes Nigeria a special place to live in is the cuisine. I do not think any country in the world has the food varieties to choose from that Nigeria has. The visual results of Google search of Nigerian cuisine—or even just talking about Nigerian foods—is enough to trigger a chemical reaction in the stomach. In a country with such vast cultures, it should come as no surprise that there are many varieties when it comes to food. Most Nigerian foods are the food you *swallow* with a variety of soups—comprising a category of food called "swallow". Swallows include pounded yam, fufu (aka *apu*), semovita, *tuwon shinkafa, amala,* and *eba.* Eba is made from crushed and air-fried cassava and often referred to as *garri* by the people from the eastern part of the country. Garri is like flour grains; you can soak it in cold water and snack on it like you would do cornflakes (some Nigerians refer to garri as *cassavaflakes*). Garri on the rocks (with ice cubes and water) goes with groundnuts, with the options of using milk and sugar. Either way, the water of a chilled garri can take you to ecstasy. Students all over Nigeria at every level, starting from secondary school and going through grad school and postgrad school, know the enormous power of garri. Every person in Nigeria, especially students, has come to appreciate the power of garri. Garri is so special it comes with different code names. The unique names of garri are *garflakes*, g4, or garium sulphate. Having groundnut in your garri is what some Nigerians call "cool and the gang". Garri mixed with hot boiling water becomes eba, which can be eaten with any soup made in Nigeria.

There is a portion of food known as pounded yam. Pounded yam is made from boiled yam pounded with the skilful hands of the pounder (the person who pounds the yam), using a mortar and pestle. When the yam is pounded properly or properly pounded, it comes out white and smooth and ready to be engaged with any Nigerian soup. You also have a food known as amala, made from dried yam ground into a fine powder. When processed in hot water, it comes out in a dark brown colour.

There is the all-powerful "fufu" also known as "akpu" in some parts of Nigeria. It is made from cassava and goes through a process that can only be called fermentation and re-fermentation. When fufu is prepared properly, it comes out looking like its cousin (pounded yam) with a unique smell.

Then there is semovita, made from corn that is dried and ground into powder. There is also tuwon shinkafa made from ground rice.

There are also varieties when it comes to the Nigerian soups that go with the foods called swallow. There is the all-popular *egusi* soup (made from melon seed), best described as a three-dimensional soup. It can be used with all types of swallows, and it can be used to eat rice or yam. There is *ogbonor* soup, which is often made with what some locals call *oporoko* (stockfish). In some parts of Nigeria, ogbonor soup is the king of all draw soups. In the class of draw soup, there is *okra, ewedu, gbegiri*, and others that cannot be mentioned because they are secret and out of bound to non-Nigerians (just joking). There is also the popular *banga* soup. For vegetable soups, there is *efo riro, afang, edikankong*, and *ofe owerri*. If one continues on this path of Nigerian soups, one might just go ahead and write a special book just on Nigerian soups.

Nigerians can perform magic with their food. Rice can be turned into fried rice, ofada rice, and the controversial jollof rice. There is a jollof rice war or competition going on in some West African countries. Nigerians will let you know that there is no contest when it comes to which country makes the best jollof rice; their jollof rice is king. Most people from Ghana, their friendly neighbours, will be shaking their heads in disagreement.

There are also varieties of appetizers, desserts, and snacks on the Nigerian menu. There is a variety of stuff to snack on, such as *chin chin*, sausage rolls, scotch eggs, puff puff, buns, moi-moi, meat pie, fish pie, bally, plantain chips, *kulikuli*, roasted groundnut, boiled groundnut, *donkuwa*, and others. You also have meat you can snack on, like *tinko*, *kilishi* (dry jerk meat), and the almighty *suya*.

Certain foods are considered specialties, among them are goat pepper soup, cow tail pepper soup, beef pepper soup, assorted pepper soup, fish pepper soup, *isi ewu*, *nkwobi*, *asun*, *ugba*, *abacha*, and others.

When you're served a meal in Nigeria, know that it comes with all kinds of meat and fish. Always expect goat meat, cow foot, cow tail, oporoko (stockfish), *kpomo* or *pomo* or *purmor* (dry cow skin), *shakki* (beef tripe), smoked fish, dry fish, and catfish.

There are locally produced drinks to go with your food in Nigeria, drinks like *zobo* (hibiscus tea), *kunu*, and the almighty palm wine, which should not be forgotten. In Nigeria, the best breakfast is *akara* with *ogi* (pap).

CHAPTER 3

WAHALA DEY

There is much pain, sorrow, and tears in the land that is flowing (or supposed to be flowing) with milk and honey. It's a self-inflicted pain—as Nigerians would say in Pidgin English, "Na we dey do ourselves", which means "We are the cause of our own pain".

Fela Ransome Kuti, one of the greatest musicians Nigeria has produced, often used his music to address social injustice in the country. In one of his songs, he talks about how you would try to find water to drink and light (electricity) in Nigeria, and you would not find any. However, if you try to look for trouble, you will get that in abundance. Nigeria is an enigma even to Nigerians. How do you suffer from the blessings you have in abundance? There are rivers across Nigeria, yet the country struggles to provide potable drinking water for its masses.

Two major rivers flow through Nigeria; their confluence is right in the centre of the country. Global warming is the only reason Nigerians should not have access to potable water.

Given the revenues the country has historically generated from crude oil, you'd think challenges related to electrical power infrastructure should be a thing of the past. You'd also expect the country to have good roads and a good transportation network. You'd expect the country to have a great healthcare system. You'd expect most schools to have modern educational technology aids for students to learn. The only thing holding Nigeria back is Nigeria's leaders.

Nigeria, like any other developing nation, struggles to provide basic infrastructure for its citizens. However, with the wealth the country called the Giant of Africa possesses, you'd expect that access to potable water should be a given. And yet, "Ordinary water for man to drink for the town, e no dey!" (Ordinary water to drink in a town is not available!)

On the streets of major cities in Nigeria, drinking water, popularly called "pure water," is sold in small cellophane bags. The purity of these bags of water is questionable; even some bottled water from popular brands is also questionable. One of the essentials of life is water, and in Nigeria, this is no exception. Water is so essential that Nigerians are quick to remind themselves that "Water No Get Enemy" (the title of one of Fela's songs), meaning "water has no enemy". Fela, in one of his classics, said it best. "There is nothing you can do without water." Even if a loved one gets killed by water, you cannot hate on the water; you cannot make water your enemy.

Water is in abundance in Nigeria, yet most Nigerians do not have easy access to potable water. Along with other reasons, some Nigerians will agree with a foreign leader like Donald Trump (who is believed to be a racist) that their country can be called a "shithole" country. When an onyinbo calls Nigerians fools, some people in Nigeria will agree with the onyinbo man. After all, as the saying goes, "Only a fool is thirsty in the abundance of water."

Nigeria has what it takes to transform itself, like Dubai in the United Arab Emirates. Yet, Nigerians are suffering amid plenty. Water does not flow regularly from taps in most Nigerian homes. At least half of those who have pipe-borne water taps in their homes in Nigeria will reveal to you that they have experienced water shutting off while taking a shower. That is why more than 90 per cent of those homes have buckets of water in the bathroom, just in case water stops running. More than half of those who use public taps have experienced a brawl at a public tap. These brawls usually start because there is no agreement on whose turn it is to get water. Sometimes these conflicts lead to a family brawl, often called *"roughor-roughor* fight" /*raw-for-raw-for fight/*. Most people outside Nigeria can't comprehend why people may wind up with Band-Aids on their heads because of brawls over trying to get water from a public tap. Every Nigerian fully understands how that can happen. The bucket in most bathrooms in Nigeria is not just to store water; it is also used to mix hot and cold water for a warm bath. You may have a hot tap and a cold tap in the house, but electricity to warm your water is another "wahala".

Electric power supply in Nigeria is mystifying. For more than three generations, Nigerians have not been able to solve their electric power situation. People living in the Western world will not be able to comprehend the notion of not having electricity, in the absence of a major natural disaster like a hurricane or a tornado. There is a story of a woman who said she grew up knowing that electric power was not constant in Nigeria. She got married, and electric power was still not constant. She started having kids, and after she'd given birth to eight children, electric power was still not constant. All her eight children are now adults, and electric power is still not constant. The woman's kids started having kids of their own (her grandchildren), and electric power is still not constant. The woman's grandkids are about to be teenagers; light is still not constant. How does the world see Nigeria? A land with so much wealth and brilliant people, yet Nigeria cannot solve the basic problem of providing constant electricity for its citizens.

When it comes to electricity in Nigeria, every Nigerian has a story to tell; every Nigerian has a NEPA story. NEPA is an acronym for National Electric Power Authority, the government body responsible for providing electricity to every household in Nigeria before it was privatised. As a result of the epileptic supply of electricity, Nigerians say NEPA stands for "Never Expect Power Always". Even in their pain, Nigerians are forever creative with their words.

All Nigerians, at one point in their lives, have had the experience of a sudden blackout while trying to watch their favourite soap opera or a football match on TV without any warning. What often follows the blackout from lack of electricity is the frustrated scream of, "*NEEEEPA!*"

In an effort by the government to pacify Nigerians, the government emphasised that the power utility company is a PLC (public liability company). Nigerians said PLC stands for "please light candle". In some parts of Nigeria, some people have experienced three months of no electricity in their neighbourhoods. These neighbourhoods are not rural areas; they are urban settlements. Imagine not having electric power for three months! If you were in a war zone, it would be understandable.

Some Nigerians can easily tell you that, once an electric transformer blows up in your community, you will be out of power for at least a couple of weeks or even months. As a result of the epileptic power supply, some Nigerians have lost their homes to fire because they had to use candles before going to bed. Some Nigerians have also died in their sleep due to carbon monoxide inhalation, caused by the fumes from their small generator known as "I pass my neighbour". Nigerians are simply creative with words and humour to aid them in coping with their struggles. Why would you call a small power generator "I pass my neighbour"? The meaning/translation of the phrase is, "Though things are tough and I'm poor, at least I am better than my next-door neighbour". Why? I can still afford to buy a small generator, while my neighbour can only afford a candle or a lantern.

There is a story of a ten-year-old boy whose school was chosen to be part of a TV show called *Animal Game* on NTA (Nigerian Television Authority). You can imagine the excitement of being among the selected few to go on national TV. While at the TV station, the boy and every child in the studio tried extremely hard to make sure the camera captured their faces. They knew millions of people would be watching at home. You can imagine the euphoria of being on national TV for a kid who is just ten years old. After the show and on the way home in the school bus, all this kid could think of was the thought of the entire family seeing him on national TV. On getting off the school bus in his neighbourhood, all that was on his mind was to confirm that his family saw him. He ran as fast as he could to get home to ask if his mum saw him.

As soon as he got home, while the mum was still trying to say welcome home, the first set of words that came out of him were, "Mummy, you see me, you see me, you see me?!" With a smile of disappointment or pity, the mum said, "No light," meaning, "No electricity."

There was another story of a professor in "UNILAG" (University of Lagos) who was having dinner at his house. He had just been served a plate of pounded yam with egusi soup, with lots of crayfish in the soup. While enjoying his meal and watching TV at the same time, NEPA struck. The professor was in total darkness; you can imagine the interruption. He decided to proceed with his meal while in the dark. Just because there is no light (electricity), does not mean you cannot find the way to your mouth. While he was in the process of eating in the dark, a cockroach landed in his soup. Yes, I know you are cringing right now. Our dear professor crushed the roach with his crayfish while eating his dinner. As if it was all planned, just after he tasted something juicy and wondered what kind of juicy crayfish he was eating, power was restored. Behold, the professor was pulling the wings of the cockroach out of his mouth. That is how the power situation in Nigeria has touched the lives of everyone. Even the healthcare sector is also affected by a lack of stable power supply.

In the United States, which is often the standard of comparison by most Nigerians, there is a good healthcare service. However, having access to that healthcare is a major problem in America. An emergency will guarantee you immediate access to good healthcare services in the United States; what will probably kill you is the bill you get after your treatment. In Nigeria, there is no access to good healthcare services. Nothing tells you more about a country's healthcare system than the leader of a country travelling out of the country he or she is leading for healthcare check-ups in a foreign country.

In Nigeria, a hospital is a place the average Nigerian goes to die. There are so many obstacles on your way to getting healthcare during an emergency. An emergency could be a heart attack, a car accident, or a gunshot wound. Imagine being shot by armed bandits in your home, and you are still alive but need to get to the hospital. More than 99 percent of the time, Nigerians drive themselves or their loved ones to the hospital during medical emergencies. There is no emergency service number to call for an ambulance to pick you up from your home—or anywhere else, for that matter—to get you to the hospital. Nigerians only observe the arrival of EMTs (Emergency Medical Technician) at the scene of an emergency in foreign movies. If there were an ambulance, the response time of getting to your house, picking you up, and getting you to the hospital would be impractical due to the poor road network and pothole-infested roads. Also, there might be slow traffic to deal with on your way to the hospital during an emergency; do not be surprised if the traffic is caused by a police checkpoint.

If you ever make it to the hospital and you have a gunshot wound, do not be shocked if the hospital staff asks for a police report before they can attend to you. Let's assume by a miracle you do have a police report (which does not make sense), there might not be a doctor in the hospital to treat you. If you are lucky enough to have a doctor, do not be shocked when you're told there is no electric power in the hospital to enable the doctor to perform a medical operation (surgery) to treat you. There are cases where the hospital is quite equipped, even with a generator, only to find out that there is no diesel to power the generator. Then there is one more obstacle that awaits you if you ever make it through all the hurdles to the hospital—the "down payment". The ethics or laws guiding the treatment of someone with a medical emergency in Nigeria are not followed. You could be in a hospital in pain or bleeding to death and have no one attending to you. The main reason for this lack of attendance is that family or friends cannot make a down payment.

The word "operation" in the Nigerian healthcare system is a petrifying word for every Nigerian. The chances of you surviving a major operation in Nigeria are fifty-fifty (that is just being generous). As for C-sections performed in Nigeria's clinics and hospitals, you hear too many cases of women losing their lives or their babies. In some cases, both mother and child lose their lives.

These are the challenges most Nigerians face when they visit a hospital during an emergency. There are countless cases of women who've died during childbirth. In Nigeria, there are just too many obstacles and challenges for everyday Nigerians. The sad thing is this was not the case in the early years of the country's independence from the British.

Not many Nigerians will dispute all that was described above. Yet, a group of Nigerians in the diaspora was arguing about how you can still live a good life in Nigeria. As a matter of fact, there are Nigerians living a great life, to the envy of those in Western countries like the United States and the United Kingdom. Living in Nigeria is like living in a fool's paradise. If you are well off, all it takes is one emergency for you to realise that all the money in the world cannot save you. Imagine being struck by a stray bullet that is lodged in your brain. Imagine being told you need heart surgery because of a heart attack. Imagine being involved in a car accident, and you're told you have internal bleeding that must be stopped. Imagine being told you have a blood clot in your brain. Imagine being told you have a bad kidney. These are situations that test your faith in the medical system in Nigeria.

Unfortunately, this is often the time people realise or become aware of the inadequacies of the healthcare system in the country. A question among the friends was, where would you rather be if you were faced with a challenging medical situation, Nigeria or abroad?

CHAPTER 4

POWER SHOW, NA ROUGH SHOW

In one of his songs, a Nigerian reggae artist known as Ras Kimono said, "Nigerians are under pressure." Nigerians are under pressure—not just the pressure of everyday economic struggle but also from the very government that is supposed to protect them. The government has brought much tears, blood, and sorrow (their regular trademarks) to Nigerians through law enforcement (LE). LE agents are notorious for using excessive force on their fellow citizens. Nigerian police are known to solicit—or, should I say, demand—bribes from their fellow citizens. It's such a common sight on the roads and the highways that it's the norm. Instead of calling it a bribe, there are many fancy names and phrases, among them "settle", "Roger", and "find something". All these fancy names are popularly called *egunje*! As a great friend (Goodman Shodeinde) explained, egunje is a bribe. "Won ti gun ki won to je" (They pound it before eating it). But *egun* can also mean something small. *Gbemu* is the opposite of egun. If someone gives you gbemu, your life can be transformed. Gbemu is the big chop, while egunje is the small chop for the police. If bribery was the only thing law enforcement officers were engaged in, Nigerians would not mind. But they also have to contend with the brutality of their LE officers.

There are countless stories of Nigerians being brutalised by law enforcement officers or getting shot to death because they refused to give bribes to the policemen who demanded them at a checkpoint. There are too many cases of accidental discharges of guns at police checkpoints, leading to the deaths of innocent Nigerians—all because of a bribe that is less than one dollar. The police in Nigeria "can do and undo" like the Nigerians say or, as Fela Kuti calls it, put on a "power show". They have too much unmonitored power. The police can arrest you without cause or justification. They search people unlawfully; they are quick to beat-up Nigerians when Nigerians dare to challenge their unlawful acts. It is a power show when you encounter an LE officer in Nigeria.

Just like in the United States of America, where African Americans do not trust the police, Nigerians do not trust their police, and they do not like the police either. For some Nigerians, it is like living in an apartheid system. The police will sometime go to where people are hanging out (most times at a local bar) and arrest everyone for no just cause. All they have to say to you is that you are a suspect. The only way you're released is when you part with a sum of money as "bail".

Every grown Nigerian has a police story to tell. There was a story in the late '80s of a man who arrived in Nigeria from the United States in the middle of the night, after a long year of absence from Nigeria. He got a cab to get him to the nearest police station just to spend the night as a safety measure because armed bandits were usually operating on the highway in the middle of the night. The man's visit to the police station was the last time anyone heard from him. The policemen at the station (Makinde Police Station, in Mafoluku, Oshodi/Isolo local government area) robbed and killed him. If not thanks to the cab driver who dropped the man at the station the night before, no one would have known about this heinous crime.

Occasionally (though not very often), Nigerians stand up against the police in public when the police have gone way out of bounds and misused their "assumed" power. There was a story of how people stood up to the police, and all the police could say to the people who stood up to them was that they were lucky they were not in the bush (isolated area), or it would have been a different story entirely. This is how I describe the Nigerian police:

P—Polite, they are not

O—Organised, they are not

L—Loving, they are not

I—Intelligent, they are not

C—Caring, they are not

E—Execution of human life, that is their specialty

The stories of Nigerian police are endless. How is that you can call a police station during an emergency, and the police will inform you that they do not have gas in their vehicle to respond to your emergency? How do you survive in a place where the police can delay their response for hours with no just cause? How do you survive in a place where the police will demand money from you before letting you go for a crime you did not commit? How do you survive in a place where the police cannot be investigated for their crimes? The police are your friends, they say; I say, "Yes, they are your friends indeed!"

Majek Fashek was right in one of his songs, "Police Brutality". He sang about police brutality and how law enforcement officers kill innocent souls. "They dem shoot, they dem kill all the leaders of tomorrow." Majek further said the insanity has caused disunity in his community. Instead of the police killing or apprehending the armed robbers, they kill the sufferers (poor innocent Nigerians).

By the way, most Nigerians do not know the number to call in case of an emergency. Even an ad for the police on the radio did not inform people how to get in touch with the police. The ad goes something like this: "Make una call police oh, armed robber no be spirit na human being like you and me. If you see anything bad just call police. Call, call, call police oh!"

You would think the add, at some point, would mention the number to call. Yet throughout the entire radio ad, no number was mentioned. All that was said was that you should call the police. That is something Nigerians should think about. I call that insanity!

Law enforcement officers are the highest lawbreakers in Nigeria. Those who are in uniform in Nigeria act like mini gods. In Nigeria, you see an LE officer driving against traffic, violating all traffic rules, and smashing the vehicles of those who have the right of way, with no consequences for their actions. In Nigeria, an LE officer will not join a queue for anything. In addition, a Nigerian LE officer will slap a person in the face for trying to express their view. In Nigeria, an LE officer will kill an innocent Nigerian, and there is no consequence for such action (and maybe that's true in the United States too). In Nigeria, LE officers can arrest you for no just cause and throw you in jail without any due process. The issue of human rights in Nigeria is just lip service. Animals in the United States are known to have more rights and privileges than Nigerian citizens have in Nigeria (and more than some Americans have in their own country).

When it comes to brutality by law enforcement agents in Nigeria, Nigerian soldiers are on a different level. Just like the police, they beat their citizens without mercy. Why would a special police task force (mobile police) be called "Kill and Go" (meaning they can kill with no accountability)? Nigerian soldiers are also called "Zombies".

A man that was in the best position to describe the atrocity of both the Nigerian police officer and the Nigerian soldier was Fela. He was brutalised at the hands of the Nigerian police while in prison. And his mom, who was over seventy years old, was thrown out of the window of a three-story building by Nigerian soldiers.

Nigerians still deal with brutality at the hands of law enforcement officer every day. It is a "rough show" for Nigerians, who are constantly under pressure.

CHAPTER 5

NA WAH!

Nigerians believe in themselves but not as much as they believe in the "oyinbo man" (white man or white woman). An oyinbo man can do no wrong in Nigeria, and the oyinbos know it all. Unfortunately, a large segment of the Nigerian population shows more respect to an oyinbo than to their fellow countrymen. There is a common belief by some Nigerians that the oyinbo knows better than them. Why would Fela go out of his way in one of his songs to say, "Oyinbo no know pass me" (The white man does not know more than me)? LE enforcement officers in Nigeria would treat oyinbo better than they do their fellow citizens.

It is safe to say that "colonial mentality is mental slavery". Mental slavery is worse than physical slavery, and some Nigerians are yet to free themselves from mental slavery. However, there is a trend that seems like some of the new generations are gradually breaking free from colonial mentality, thanks to many Nigerians who have lived and studied abroad and are now back in the country "doing things" (as Nigerians would say).

Bob Marley said, "Emancipate yourselves from mental slavery. None but ourselves can free our minds." Nigerians are yet to fully grasp the importance of that mindset. Just like the effects of slavery in America, the effects of colonial mentality in Nigeria run deep. The result of colonial mentality is that you believe the oyinbo man is better than you. you might consider yourself a Pan-Africanist, but in your subconscious, you still prefer that the oyinbo man handle certain situations.

Some Nigerians pride themselves on those words of Fela, "Oyinbo no know pass me". Some Nigerians come to the realisation of their worth when they have lived in the Western world. When you study with oyinbo and your test scores are much higher than those of your oyinbo counterparts, that is when you say to yourself, *Oyinbo no know pass me*. The mere fact that a person must seek validation for him or herself by comparing test scores with an oyinbo person is a product of colonial mentality. The most popular way some Nigerians express their colonial mentality is when they take pictures in a foreign land and place an oyinbo in the picture so they can pridefully show it to their friends and families back home.

The colonial mentality in the psyche of Nigerians runs deep. When you visit Nigeria with your oyinbo counterpart, everyone automatically assumes the oyinbo is the "oga" (boss). Nigerians show more care to the foreigner whose skin pigment is much lighter than theirs than they do their fellow Nigerians. The oyinbo is treated much better by the police than the locals are. Some Nigerians prefer that an oyinbo coach the national football team because they've been subdued into believing the oyinbo knows better. Unfortunately, certain events reinforce that mentality. When Nigeria took the gold medal in soccer in the USA '96 Olympics, such a notion was reinforced because the coach was an oyinbo man (Jo Bonfrère). Nigerians are willing to take a chance on or give an oyinbo an opportunity they will never give to a fellow Nigerian.

A few Nigerians remember the failure of the Nigerian Eagles (national soccer team) on the way to the USA '96 Olympics. Most

Nigerians, if not all, had written off the Eagles because of a friendly match played in Lagos. The Eagles lost a friendly match to a team they had no business losing to. If Nigerians kept records, it would be easy to remember the team. Somehow, the Nigerian Football Association left the oyinbo coach still managing the team. I bet, if the coach were a Nigerian, he would have been fired.

However, some Nigerians to date do not believe the coach got Nigeria the victory of the Olympic gold medal in the United States. Many Nigerians believe it was the sheer will, skills, and talents of the players that brought Nigeria that glory. If Nigerians kept records, they would all remember the Nigerian coach (Shuaibu Amodu) who went to South Africa and took a club known as Orlando Pirates to victory and made the team a national champion in the South African league. If we had records, we would have noticed that he proved himself in Nigeria first, when he took the football club known as Lions of Gboko to victory by winning the FA Cup in Nigeria. Shuaibu Amodu qualified for the Nigerian national team twice (2002 and 2010) to the FIFA Men's World Cup. Few Nigerians remember when Nigeria was on the verge of not qualifying for the world cup and an oyinbo coach was fired and replaced by Shuaibu Amodu. Amid hopelessness, a Nigerian coach led Nigeria to qualify for the world cup. How did the Nigeria FA (football association) pay him back? By firing him before the start of the World Cup he'd led Nigeria to qualify for, all because he had a spat with the minister of sport. I'd bet if Shuaibu Amodu was an oyinbo person, he would not have been fired by the Nigerian Football Association.

The Oyinbo man will always enjoy preference in Nigeria; that is why, in all the multinational companies in Nigeria, rarely will you see a Nigerian as the top man in that company. There is always one oyinbo ahead of the Nigerians. What the oyinbo will not accept in his country

Nigerians will allow to happen in Nigeria. That is the power of the colonial mentality! Some Nigerians might think they have broken out of that chain, but in certain situations, Nigerians remain victims of colonial mentality. Imagine needing to have a brain or heart surgery, and you are given the option to choose between an oyinbo doctor (a foreign doctor) or a Nigerian doctor trained in the West. Who would you choose? Take your time to think about that.

Nigerians do not value their ideas till an oyinbo man implements those same ideas. The Western countries know how to repackage things originally from Africa as their own. It is only when stuff from Africa is repackaged that Africans show appreciation. Old folks in Nigeria are known to have tattoos on their bodies; nobody paid attention until people from Western countries started adding colours to the same tattoos that originated from the motherland. Nigerian and African attire got little or no attention till Nigerians saw how this attire was rocked in the blockbuster movie *Black Panther*. Nigerians have a fight sport called *gidigbo* in the Yoruba language and *dambe* in Hausa. They paid little or no attention to it till people in the West turned it into MMA fighting. Many games could be made into multimillion-naira businesses, but Nigerians won't appreciate them until an oyinbo does it. It's all about packaging. I guess Nigerians love to copy the Western countries because nobody will pay attention to an idea originally generated in Nigeria. TV shows like *Gulder Ultimate Search* sponsored by Nigerian Breweries, *Housewives of Lekki*, and *Nigerian Idol* are all examples of TV shows copied from the West.

Colonial mentality makes Nigerians believe a person who speaks phonetics or *phornne* (as Nigerians call it) is more intelligent than a person who cannot speak proper or fluent English. It is colonial mentality that makes some Nigerian newscasters and actors want to speak through their noses. In some parts of Nigeria, native names are considered names of an infidel, while religious names from the two most popular religions are considered names from God or Allah. As Nigerians often say, "Na wah!"

There is also the issue of pay disparity between qualified Nigerians and their oyinbo counterparts in Nigeria. That is a different matter entirely, though. I guess this is what would make most Nigerians say, "Nawawa wah!"

You often hear a Nigerian say, "Na wah!" It is an exclamation for something shocking or surprising. The challenge every Nigerian faces amid plenty is mind-boggling (it's a na wah situation). The land is blessed, flowing with milk and honey, and yet, people are suffering. There is no situation that more truly paints Nigerians suffering amid plenty than the situation of petrol scarcity. In what world would a country be among the leading producers of a product, exporting that product to the rest of the world, yet the citizens of that country are constantly facing scarcity of that same product?

The pain and discomfort Nigerians endure is unbelievable. There is a saying that, if you push Nigerians into a corner or up against a wall, they do not fight back; they simply jump over the wall. Religious beliefs have taught Nigerians how to endure and not to fight back. Nigerians are taught to have faith and belief because God or Allah will make it better someday.

Nigerians seem helpless when it comes to challenging their government, helpless to fight for what is right, and helpless to fight for their human rights. The question is, How should Nigerians fight back? In the past, Nigeria had leaders who spoke out against bad government policies. Those who come to mind include Fela Anikulapo Kuti, Beko

Kuti, and Gani Fawehinmi. In modern times, it seems those leaders no longer exist. In present-day Nigeria, the question is, Who is Nigeria's Gandhi? Who is Nigeria's Malcolm X? Who is Nigeria's Martin Luther King Jr?

The Nigerian system seems to have made Nigerians tougher, more tolerant, and more patient than ever. Nigerians have been trained to never give up. The Nigerian Mantra is, "Just because it is raining today does not mean the sun will not shine tomorrow." The Nigerian system has made Nigerians adapt to any form of inconvenience and unnecessary difficulty. The Nigerian system is a system where you expect that things will not work smoothly or correctly by default. The Nigerian system is a system where one is made to expect that, if you need any service from the government or private entity, you must be ready to grease an itchy palm. The Nigerian system is operated to expect frustration in what is a simple process in other parts of the world. The Nigerian system is operated to expect delay and to experience what Fela called "go slow".

Tears and pain and blood have made Nigerians highly creative when it comes how they communicate—their organically grown style of communication (Nigerian Pidgin English) a coping mechanism. Nigerians are built to survive. Where else in the world would you have an irregular power supply, lack of emergency response, lack of good medical facilities, and lack of quality government regulations and people remain sane? Where else are the police free to openly extort money from people on the streets and abuse the country's citizens physically, and people are still able to keep their sanity? In some other countries, the people would have declared war if they were faced with half of the challenges Nigerians face in their own country—that or there would be a rise in mental health cases.

Many Nigerians have given up hope that life will ever get better in Nigeria, though a few still believe it will be better one day. The painful thing about Nigeria is that life used to be great. As time passes, things seem to be getting worse for most people. Despite all that has been said, a few Nigerians are living like kings.

CHAPTER 6

FAJI PEOPLE

Nigeria's national anthem says, "The labour of our heroe's past shall never be in vain." Ah ah! (a general exclamation from the people in the western part of Nigeria when they are about to disagree with someone or when they hear something unbelievable). If you ask me, I say Nigerians have forgotten the labour of their heroes past. Nigeria does not have an archive to keep a proper record of its history. Most of the youth do not know the heroes or "sheroes" of yesteryears. If you asked who Nigeria's first prime minister was (Sir Abubakar Tafawa Belawa), not too many youth know the answer to that question today. Thanks to Google, people now have information close at their fingertips (even at that, the information is succinct). How many Nigerians know where the first prime minister was buried? How many Nigerians know where the first prime minister was from? What do Nigerians know about Dr Nnamdi Azikiwe? What do Nigerians know about Queen Amina of Zaria? What do Nigerians know about Herbert Macaulay? What do Nigerians know about King Jaja of Opobo?

Nigerians do not seem to care about thoroughly documenting their past or history! There used to be a great show on national television in Nigeria (NTA) called *The Village Headmaster*. An unconfirmed rumour in Nigeria is that the tapes of the recorded shows were all burnt by the manager of the TV station. There are also rumours that some members of the staff of the TV station recorded over the tapes. This kind of hearsay in Nigeria is called "dem say" (it means, "I do not know how true the story is, but this is the rumour, whose source I don't know).

Where are the TV shows from yesteryears? I'm talking about shows like:

- *Adio Family*
- *Village Headmaster*
- *Winds against My Soul*
- *For Better for Worse*
- *New Masquerade*
- *Koco Close*
- *Basi and Company*
- *Second Chance*
- *Cock Crow at Dawn*
- *Mirror in the Sun*
- *Ripples*
- *Checkmate*

Where are they? Nigerians do not see reruns of all these shows on their local television.

There are TV writers and movie producers who made their mark in Nigeria, like Chief Hubert Adedeji Ogunde, Jimmy Odumosu, Lola Fani-Kayode, and Tade Ogidan. In today's Nigeria, there seem to be no records of the works of these actors and writers.

And what about great Nigerian actors of yesteryears? A list would include:

- Jab Adu (Dr Bassey Okon in *Village Headmaster*)
- Ted Mukoro (headmaster in *Village Headmaster*)
- Femi Robinson (headmaster in *Village Headmaster*)
- Justice Esiri (headmaster in *Village Headmaster*)
- Dejumo Lewis (Kabiyesi or Olaja in *Village Headmaster*)
- Joe Layode (teacher in *Village Headmaster*)
- Oba Funsho Adeolu (Chief Eleyinmi in *Village Headmaster*)
- Ibidun Allison (Amebo in *Village Headmaster*)
- Elsie Olushola (Sisi Clara in *Village Headmaster*)
- Albert Kosemani Olayemi (Gorimapa in *Village Headmaster*)
- Sunday Omobolanle (Papiluwe or Aluw)
- Geroge Menta (Bello in *Cockcrow at Dawn*)
- Ene Onoja (Zeweye in *Cockcrow at Dawn*)
- Sadiq Daba (Bitrus in *Cockcrow at Dawn*)
- Kasimu Yaro (Uncle Gaga in *Cockcrow at Dawn*)
- Femi Jarrett (Uncle Alagbin in *Adio Family*)
- Moses Olaiya (Baba Sala)
- Tunji Oyelana (Sura the tailor)
- Olumide Bakara (Chief Koko in *Koko Close*)

And there are many more! Where are they now?

Some of these actors are dead, and their works will never be remembered. Their works have been lost and forgotten in the Nigerian history of art. I bet most Nigerians know much about past foreign actors like Clint Eastwood and Roger Moore. And yet, they have no idea who the above-listed actors were. Those are the people Nigerians should honour. They were the pioneers. Despite the challenges and the troubles,

Nigeria is the birthplace of the following people who have made their marks on the world stage:

Name	Area of distinction	For
Fela Anikulapo Kuti	Afrobeat	Known as the king/ originator of Afrobeat
Sade Adu	Music	Grammy Award winner
Prof. Wole Soyinka	Literature	Nobel laureate in literature
Hakeem Olajuwon	Sports (basketball)	Basketball and NBA champion
Chinua Achebe	Literature	A great poet and novelist.
Dr Bennet Omalu	Medical neuropathology	A renowned medical doctor and the subject of a movie starring Will Smith, *Concussion* (2015)
Taiwo Ajayi Lycett	Media	International TV icon
Oludotun Jacobs (aka Olu Jacobs)	Media	International TV icon
Bolaji Badejo	Art and media	Visual artist and actor
Orlando Martins	Media and theatre	Pioneering film and stage actor
Richard Ihetu (Dick Tiger)	Athletics (boxing)	World middleweight and lightweight champion
Samuel Okon Peters	Athletics (boxing)	World Boxing Council heavyweight champion
Nojim Maiyegun	Athletics (boxing)	First Olympic bronze medal winner for Nigeria
Peter Konyegwachie	Athletics (boxing)	First Olympic silver medal winner for Nigeria
Chioma Ajunwa-Opara (aka Chioma Ajunwa)	Athletics (long jump)	First Olympic gold medal winner for Nigeria

Abiodun Obafemi, Augustine Okocha (Jay Jay), Celestine Babayaro, Daniel Amokachi (the Bull), Emmanuel Amuneke, Emmanuel Babayaro, Garba Lawal, Joseph Dosu, Nwanko Kanu, Kingsley Obiekwu, Mobi Obaraku, Uche Mbamaoneyeukwu, Sunday Oliseh, Taribo West Teslim, Tijani Babangida, Victor Ikepba and Wilson Oruma	Sports (football or soccer)	First Olympic gold medal winners in a team sport for Nigeria
Chimamanda Ngozi Adichi	Literature	An acclaimed non-fiction writer
Maasai Ujiri	Sports (basketball)	Manager of NBA champion team (Toronto Raptors)
Philip Emeagwali	Computing and mathematics	Winner of the 1989 Gordon Bell Prize for an application of the CM-2 massively-parallel computer

There are people in the world whose lineage began in Nigeria, including:

Name	Area of Distinction
Seal (Henry Olusegun Adeola Samuel)	Music / Grammy award winner
Adewale Akinnuoye-Agbaje	Movies / Hollywood actor
Chiwetel Ejiofor	Movies / Hollywood actor
David Oyelowo	Movies / Hollywood actor
John Boyega	Movies / Hollywood actor

Hakeem Kae-Kazim	Movies / Hollywood actor
Andre Tyler Iguodala	NBA champion
Festus Ezeli	NBA champion
Victor Oladipo	NBA champion
Giannis Antetokounmpo	NBA champion
Al-Farouq Aminu	NBA champion

And there are many more!

Nigeria is a country where every child is taught about the value of education; as a child in Nigeria, you are told to be a doctor, a lawyer, or an engineer. Unfortunately, not every kid in Nigeria gets to be any of these. It is better to have a good education than to have money, as education brings you money. Simply put, it is better to be educated than to be rich. That might be changing in today's Nigeria, with Nigerian music going global.

Nigerians cannot explain their excitement when they hear a Nigerian Afro hip-hop song playing on American pop and R&B radio stations. Nigerian hip-hop artists have put Nigerian music back on the global musical map. In today's Nigeria, you have young artists whose music is making waves all over the world. The likes of 2Face, Don Jazzy, D'banji, Burna Boy, Wizkid, Davido, Tiwa Savage, Tekno, Timaya, Banky W, and many more are making Nigeria proud despite the challenges they face in Nigeria. Nigerian songs are frequently played in night clubs across the country and outside Nigeria (this was not the case in the past).

This is how I see Nigeria, a place where the people are:

N—Nice
I—Intelligent
G—Generous
E—Energetic
R—Reliable
I—Indomitable
A—Adorable

Nigerians are highly creative people; they can smile through their pain and suffering despite the challenges they face every day. Nigerians who were in secondary school in the '80s had the wonderful pleasure of experiencing comic magazines like *Lolly* and *Ikebe Super*. The creation of the characters in these magazines had a profound effect on every Nigerian who had the pleasure of reading them. That is the genius and creative mind of the average Nigerian. Where in the world would someone come up with the idea of these characters? Characters like Papa Ajasco, Pa Jimoh, Buy Alinco, and Miss Pepeye are all created by a man called Wale Adenuga. These fictitious characters could only come from someone who has a creative mind.

Papa Ajasco of *Ikeba Super* is a married old man, probably in his sixties who loves ladies. He is what you would call a sugar daddy. Unlike Dauda, the sexy guy (description below), he is a bit discrete with his affairs with the ladies. He is bald and often has a pair of reading glasses barely hanging over his nose. Papa Ajasco is shameless and filled with different schemes on how to get the attention of the ladies.

Pa Jimoh is a wretched old man who was often duped because he was naive. He is often clueless as to what's going on around him. Simply put, he is an old fool.

Boy Alinco, on the hand, is a smart savvy guy. He sees himself as a ladies' man. Boy Alinco is always involved in a scheme to either make money or get the ladies' attention.

Miss Pepeye is a classy lady who often ends up with the wrong man. Looking back now, she would be the feminist of her time.

Lolly, the magazine that featured a fictitious character known as Dauda, the Sexy Guy, was created by someone from the northern part of Nigeria (I remain uncertain on further details), which is a very conservative part of the country. The funny thing about Dauda of *Lolly* is that he was not sexy-looking. The character became so popular in Nigeria that people who were named Dauda became uncomfortable with their given names. Dauda, the Sexy Guy was practically a rapist if you ask the opinion of some Nigerians today. He was constantly ready to sleep with any woman he set his eyes on. A lady better not drop her guard in public, or else Dauda would strike. No matter the size of the woman, Dauda had the strength to carry the woman and run. As the magazine became popular, there were rumours of protest about the character called Dauda. The name Dauda is a popular name among the people of northern Nigeria. If there ever was a protest of the use of the name Dauda, it must have worked because the name of the character was later changed to Nackson. In Nigeria, when you hear a man say, "I nack that woman", it means he had sex with the woman. "Nacking" means banging (a Nigerian Pidgin English word for sex). The last I heard about Dauda, aka Nackson, he is now a conservative religious individual (just joking).

In present Nigeria, up and coming comedians do not have to look up to Eddie Murphy and Dave Chapple. Young comedians have comedians such as Ali Baba, Julius Agwu, Okey Bakassi, Sheyi Law, Helen Paul, WarriPikin, Basket Mouth, I Go Die, I Go Save, Sim Card, A Y (aka

Ayo Makun), Bovi, Gordons, Akpororo (aka Ahpo-ro-ro)– just to name
a few—to look up to.

If you ask me, every Nigerian is a comedian. Life in Nigeria is
comedy! If you grew up in certain poor neighbourhoods, life in those
neighbourhoods is a comedy. If you grew up in a military barracks in
Nigeria, life in the barracks is a comedy. There are more than enough
comic materials in your environment to provide comedy. If you need
comic material in Nigeria, just hop onto a public transportation bus
known as "Molue", and you will have enough material for a lifetime.

PART III

100 COMMON EXPRESSIONS WITH WISDOM

CHAPTER 7

WISDOM

1. **Dey say church don burn down finish with Father inside, you dey ask whether Father get biabia.**

   Translation: They said a church just burned down with the priest inside, and you are asking whether the priest had a beard.

   Interpretation: You are asking an irrelevant question amid a more serious issue.

   When such a statement comes up in a conversation among Nigerians, they are trying to say that someone is saying something that is not relevant to the subject or topic of discussion. A good example of this would be someone talking about a car accident that resulted in the death of a baby inside the car and someone inquiring about the gender of the baby.

2. **Na only when lion wound, antelope dey remember say lion dey owe am money.**

   Translation: Only when the lion is seriously injured does the antelope remember it has a debt to collect from the lion.

Interpretation: You only confront those you fear when they are most vulnerable or weak.

It is the norm to show respect to people who are in the position of power; because of the powerful position, you often can't speak truth to power. However, once the person in power loses that position, you soon realise you can confront that person without fear of any consequence.

3. **Na big name dey kill dog.**

Translation: A big name kills the dog.

Interpretation: Pretending to be rich while you are poor or pretending to be what you are not will lead to pain or to your demise.

In Nigeria, people love showing off, and they also love to be acknowledged. You will often see a man buying drinks for everyone at a bar for a celebration or just because he can. However, the man buying drinks for everyone might not be well off financially. A typical case of "a big name kills the dog" is a guy trying to impress a girl by lavishing her with stuff while being in a very tough financial situation.

4. **Wetin concern agbero with overload?**

Translation: Is the motor park tout concerned about excessive luggage?

Interpretation: Why is that my business or my concern?

Touts are often called *agbero* in Nigeria. You will easily find them at the car parks and airports. A tout is only concerned about money—nothing else matters. If a tout is asked to load up a vehicle, he couldn't care less if the load or luggage will do any damage to the vehicle. The tout has one and only one concern, which is getting the luggage in the vehicle.

In a country with so many pressing issues, you often find yourself in a conversation that you really do not care about. While the issue being discussed might be an important one, it is just not of concern to you at the moment, because it has no direct implication for you. *Wetin concern agbero with overload?* is a rhetorical question. If the United States is planning on going to war with their usual suspect (Iran), while the war might have a global implication, it's just not a concern to a person who lives in Nigeria. Since there is no direct or immediate effect, the person in Nigeria is not concerned about the war.

5.   **Na only chewing stick know the secret of mouth.**

Translation: Only your toothbrush knows where it hurts in your mouth.

Interpretation: Only those who are close to you know your secret.

People often have personal problems that are hard for them to share with their close friends and families. However, there may be one or two people close to you who are aware of your challenges. A woman might not be happy because of her husband's sexual performance in the "other room" (the bedroom). As a result, she is often seen by others as a woman who doesn't smile. Only those with whom she has shared her secret know her pain.

6. **Na from clap, dance dey take start.**

Translation: A clap of the hand precedes a dance.

Interpretation: There is a preceding action before the main action.

There is always a prelude before a main event; Nigerians believe there is always a sign before something major happens. If a man is toasting a woman—trying to ask her out—and the woman is full of smiles, that is a sign she will likely give in to his intention towards her. Conversely, if a girl doesn't like you, there are signs given before she tells you no!

7. **No be how person talk take borrow money, e dey talk when e wan pay.**

Translation: The way you talk when you are about to borrow money is not the same way you talk when it's time for you to pay up.

Interpretation: The way we behave when we are in need is totally different to when we are not in need.

It is just human nature; when you're in desperate need for something, which is often money in Nigeria, your demeanour is usually sombre. However, when you start making lots of money, there is usually an arrogance in your demeanour. There is arrogance in your behaviour when you have money, and there is humility in your behaviour when you don't have money.

8. **Wetin concern craze man with doctor?**

Translation: What business does a psychiatric patient have with a gynaecologist?

Interpretation: Why is that my business?

This is also a rhetorical question. Nigerians often use this question to communicate that they have no business with what you are communicating to them. When a piece of information that is being passed to you is of no value, and you want to dismiss that information, this expression is quite common.

9. **No be every rain wey fall dey touch person.**

Translation: Not every rainfall touches you.

Interpretation: You are not supposed to know about every bit of information.

When grown folks are having a conversation, and a younger person wants to know what the conversation is all about, you might be told *no be every rain wey fall dey touch you*. It is a simple way of saying mind your business. This is often said to people who are very nosy.

10. **Na chief wey e no know himself dey go dance disco dance with small children during ceremony.**

Translation: A chief who is not aware of his status or position is the one who dances with little kids at a party.

Interpretation: When you don't know your place, you end up at a place beneath you.

This statement is usually a reference to a person who doesn't respect him or herself. When you don't respect yourself, you end up not being respected.

11. **That one na only for home video e dey happen.**

Translation: That only happens in the movies

Interpretation: The situation or event is not realistic.

When a story is unbelievable to a Nigerian, you will often hear such a statement.

12. **The egbo wey person smoke wey clear him brain, na him another person smoke wey make am run mad.**

Translation: The same marijuana a person smokes and gets inspiration from will cause mental issues for another.

Interpretation: What is good for someone may be dangerous for others.

There are certain processes that work well for some people but are detrimental to others.

13. **Pikin wey say him mama no go sleep, him sef no go sleep.**

Translation: A child who says the mother will not sleep will also not sleep.

Interpretation: If you try to cause a problem for others, you too will have problems in your life.

Not much explanation is needed here; if you go around disturbing people's peace of mind, you will not have peace yourself. Nigerians believe in karma. What goes around comes around.

14. **Na for old age ashawo they cry for pikin.**

Translation: Only at old age does a prostitute yearn for a baby.

Interpretation: Only when you've past your prime do you regret not achieving what you were supposed to have achieved in your youth.

When you are young, you often feel like you have all the time in the world. As you get much older, you begin to reflect on the things you should have done or achieved when you were younger.

15. **Monkey no fine, but im mama like am.**

Translation: A monkey is not beautiful, yet it is loved by its mother.

Interpretation: You are not perfect in the eyes of the world, but you are still loved by those close to you.

Your look, your actions, your behaviour, or your attitude might not please the people you encounter, but to those remarkably close to you, you are simply fine.

16. **Cow wey no get tail, na God day pursue fly for am.**

Translation: A cow with no tail has only God to help it keep flies away from its body.

Interpretation: Only God provides for those who are in need.

In a country like Nigeria, where people are deeply religious, there is a belief that God does not forget his people. Sometimes, people wonder how they survive daily in a country where the unemployment rate is extremely high and where there is no access to quality health care services. Yet, people are not only surviving but also thriving.

17. **Na eye person take dey know pounded yam wey go belle full am.**

Translation: You use your eyes in gauging the amount of pounded yam that will satisfy you.

Interpretation: You use your senses to know your ability or your limit.

If you are going to engage in a fight with someone, one important decision is to access the strength of the person you're going to engage before you strike.

18. **Nah by style, guy dey take tell im mama to close her nyash.**

Translation: You find a unique way to inform your mother that her private part is showing when she is in public.

Interpretation: You don't openly communicate sensitive information to your parents, to your family members, or to your close friends in public. A coded way or language is used to communicate sensitive information.

It is customary for older mothers in Nigeria to wear what is popularly called a wrapper. This is just a piece of cloth wrapped around the waist. Most times, these women sit on a stool, and because of the way they are seated, you can see between their legs. Now imagine your mum having a conversation with her friends, and she is exposed. How do you tell her that what should be private is exposed? You can't do that openly; a wise child will do that discreetly.

19. **I no gree, I no gree, na im dey tear shirt.**

Translation: I won't tolerate this; I won't tolerate that is how a shirt gets ripped off.

Interpretation: Disagreement often leads to a fight.

Often, a disagreement between two people leads to a conflict. As a result of the conflict, clothing gets ripped off. In essence, failing to come to an agreement during a dispute will lead to a conflict. There is often a loss of something of value during a conflict. In Nigeria, where people are under pressure from the hardship of life, a small dispute often will lead to a major conflict because of the already pervading frustration.

20. **Na small, na im crayfish take enter soup.**

Translation: Gradually, that is how crayfish makes its way into the soup.

Interpretation: A situation that becomes a crisis often builds up gradually.

When Nigerians say *small small*, what they are saying is, Take it easy; be gradual or be gentle. Crayfish is used to make stew, and our beloved jollof rice. The soup is a metaphor for a tough situation; this makes sense because soup is usually hot before being consumed. *Na small small, na im crayfish take enter soup* is often a warning or caution. Ordinarily, a fish on its own will not dive into a hot soup.

21. If you like turn around 100 times, your nyash go still dey back.

Translation: If you turn around 100 times, your buttocks will always be behind you.

Interpretation: Certain things will never change, no matter how you try to dress them up.

In Nigeria, certain things will never change; no matter how many times we try to reform them, they just stay the same. There are many examples of situations not changing in Nigeria despite effort and a push for change. There have been many efforts toward making the electric power supply constant in Nigeria; despite such actions over the years, the electric power situation in Nigeria is still the same (epileptic).

The Nigerian Police Force is another example of things that have not changed. Despite the change in uniform in the years past, and despite the reform the force has undergone, the police are still ineffective, and roadside bribery or extortion of motorists is still ongoing.

Also, Nigerian politicians are known to change parties after every election (carpet crossing); they act corruptly. All the people have to do is listen to some of Fela's songs and realise that things have not changed much for the better in Nigeria.

22. Soup wey sweet, na money kill am.

Translation: Soup that is sweet, it is money that killed it.

Interpretation: Delicious soup is achieved by good money spent on making the soup.

A quality product is the result of good money spent or invested.

Anything of good quality comes with a hefty price; in Nigeria, that is a common belief. When an older woman is looking beautiful and looks much younger than her age, you often hear people in Nigeria say that expression. Literally, if you make a good soup that is tasty, such expression is also used. In a society where it costs so much to feed people, when a man complains that his wife's cooking is not good, he will be quickly reminded by his wife that more money will make her prepare a better meal. This is rephrased as *better soup, na money kill am*.

23. Shine your eye!

Translation: Shine your eyes.

Interpretation: This simply means be smart. It also means be extremely cautious.

Nigerians are known to be book-smart; however, they are also street-smart. There is a general belief that, to survive in life, you need to be both book-smart and street-smart. When Nigerians talk about *shine your eye*, it is usually in reference to being street-smart. If you are moving into a new city or territory you are not familiar with, you will often be told by close associates to *shine your eye*. This simply means to be careful, so that you are not swindled. A man will often be told to shine his eye by his close friends or associates if they believe a woman is about to outsmart him. Also, if a business proposition is suspected to be fraudulent, friends and associates will tell you to *shine your eye*.

24. Woman wey dey find pikin no dey waer pant go sleep.

Translation: A woman who wants to have a baby or is planning to get pregnant does not go to bed wearing her underwear.

Interpretation: When you need something badly, you do not let anything be an obstacle to achieving it. Anything that will be a hindrance to achieving your goal must be put aside.

I don't think this statement needs further explanation; this statement is pretty clear as it is. A woman who is trying to get pregnant at all costs will rarely say she is not in the mood to make love to her husband or partner. This statement is just a metaphor and is not specifically for women. It is about not having an obstacle in your way to achieving any goal you set for yourself. A student who wants to get a good grade on an upcoming exam should not spend most of his or her time playing; instead, he or she should be studying.

25. Any butterfly wey fly straight, e no be butterfly again.

Translation: A butterfly that is flying straight is no longer a butterfly.

Interpretation: You are no longer ordinary when you are exceptional.

A butterfly doesn't fly straight, so if it flies straight it is no longer a butterfly. There are reasons certain people are called geniuses; the title of *genius* is not for everyone. In the course of history, certain people are just exceptional in their various fields of endeavour. In Nigeria, there are many in their various fields doing exceptional work. The person that readily comes to mind in Nigeria is Fela Anikulapo Kuti. Fela, as he was popularly known, would be that butterfly who flew straight. In more ways than one, Fela was exceptional. His music was exceptional; so was his activism for the freedom of his people. The enigmatic Fela introduced Afrobeat to the world. When it came to matters of civil and human rights, he stood up in the face of the military junta in Nigeria. The Kuti clan was comprised of butterflies who flew straight.

In world history, certain people are just exceptional in their various fields of endeavour. In the world of boxing, Muhammed Ali would indeed be that butterfly who flew straight, even though he floated like one. In the world of basketball, Michael Jordan would be the butterfly who flew straight. In pop music, Michael Jackson would be the butterfly who flew straight. Malcolm X and Martin Luther King Jr were butterflies who flew straight in the '60s during the civil rights movement in America. Mahatma Gandhi was the butterfly who flew straight in India. In Jamaica, Robert Nesta Marley was the butterfly who flew straight with his music and activism for the movement of black people.

26. **"Na feel at home", dey make visitor spoil remote control.**

Translation: When a visitor is told to feel at home, he could get so carried away that he destroys the TV remote.

Interpretation: When a person gets too familiar with you or too comfortable, he or she loses respect for you and your property.

This is the Nigerian way of saying *familiarity breeds contempt.*

27. Person wey dey roast corn, no dey waka far.

Translation: A person who is roasting corn doesn't walk far away from the corn he or she is roasting.

Interpretation: If you are supervising something particularly important, you keep a close eye on what you are supervising.

Nigerians are trained to be vigilant about their surroundings or environment. In a country where some people are very fetish and you have dubious elements in society, it is not uncommon for you to be told to watch where you go and what you do. There is the belief that, if someone is envious of your success or achievement, that person will want to do you harm. People are always mindful of what they do, especially if what they are doing is considered sensitive.

28. One day monkey go market, e no go come back.

Translation: A monkey will go shopping one day and will not return

Interpretation: Someday, you will assume the responsibility of being independent.

The statement is simply a warning. An example of this in Nigeria would be a situation where you are not treating your woman right. When this statement is made, you are simply being told that your woman will walk away from you one day to never return.

29. No use pole vault jump into guy way.

Translation: Don't use a pole vault to jump into the arena of being a trendy guy.

Interpretation: Don't be in a rush.

The statement is a simple statement of caution. Most times, people live in the fast lane just to make it big in Nigeria. It's not uncommon for such a statement: *Ol' boy, take am easy, no use pole vault jump into guy way.*

30. Dem no dey tell blind man say rain dey fall.

Translation: You don't have to tell a blind man it is raining.

Interpretation: You don't have to explain something that is quite obvious, or you don't have to inform someone of an obvious impending danger.

When a Nigerian sees people running in a particular direction, he or she doesn't wait and ask why people are running. A Nigerian just joins in the direction of the crowd. Only when all is settled do you ask what is happening.

31. **No matter how goat squeeze face reach for market, person wey go buy am, go buy am.**

Translation: No matter the expression on the face of a goat, whoever wants to buy it will buy it.

Interpretation: No matter what you do, what's going to be is going to be.

Life does not care whether you are good-looking or ugly. It sure doesn't care whether you're rich or poor. Life will throw challenges at you no matter your status.

32. **E dey sweet me, e dey sweet, na im dey make old woman get belle.**

Translation: Sweet and enjoyable sexual pleasure leads to pregnancy for an old lady.

Interpretation: Excessive pleasure often leads to a negative consequence.

The statement is a warning for those who live a pleasurable life. Nigerians are known to enjoy life; despite the hardship they face, they still have a way of enjoying themselves. One way Nigerians get by the hardship of no constant power supply is spending time in the evening at a local bar to have a beer. However, excessive drinking could lead to drunk driving, which could lead to a major road accident. Excessive drinking could also lead to health issues.

Also, traditionally it is expected that a man enjoys the company of a woman, and in Nigerian this is no exception. The pleasure of a single man and a single woman engaging themselves in the "other room" sometimes lead to unwanted pregnancy.

33. **Beautiful girl wey no get sense, na her private part dey suffer am.**

Translation: A beautiful girl who is not smart will have her private part in pain due to her foolishness.

Interpretation: A beautiful girl who is swayed by the sweet promises of men will be taken advantage of.

For a young lady, beauty alone is not enough; if she is naive, men will have their way with her and take full advantage. We all know what it means for a man to take advantage of a woman.

34. **Body no be firewood.**

Translation: The human body is not firewood.

Interpretation: The human body has needs.

When a person has been deprived of sex for a while, he or she will react to an opportunity to release sexual pressure. However, you do not need to be deprived of sex for your body to respond to the touch of an admirer. Often, when people fall into temptation or find themselves in a seductive situation, you will hear Nigerians say, *My body no be firewood*—meaning their body is not a piece of wood. There is life in their body; that is why the body will respond to seduction.

35. **Na overfamiliarity (over-sabi) make, "Good morning," turn to, "How far?"**

Translation: When someone gets too familiar with you, instead of greeting you formally by saying something like, "Good morning," they say, "How far?"

Interpretation: Familiarity breeds contempt.

The Nigerian culture demands you show respect to your elders. Not greeting or acknowledging someone properly is often seen as being disrespectful. Unfortunately, when you become too close and too familiar with someone, you get carried away and end up not acknowledging the person like you are supposed to. Familiarity makes you lose all protocol.

36. **Stone wey dey for centre of the river, no dey fear rain.**

Translation: A stone in the middle of the river doesn't have the fear of rain.

Interpretation: As the popular saying goes, a man who is down on the floor fears no fall.

A student who is in medical school is not afraid of the sight of a cadaver. If you love going to the library, you should not be afraid of books. A man who loves women should not be afraid of spending money. If you love gambling, you should not be afraid to lose money.

37. Pikin wey dem carry for back, no know how far the journey be.

Translation: A child who is being carried during the entire course of a journey does not have a clue as to the distance of the journey.

Interpretation: A person who has lived a privileged life has no clue what life's hardships are all about.

In life, if you haven't gone through challenging situations, you usually don't have an idea about that experience. Nigeria is a typical case of "tales of two cities"—one of those who are very well off (often called *butter*) and another of those who are not (often called *paki* or *pako*). In life, it is often difficult for people to understand the plight of those who are struggling. A child in the Western world will never understand what it means not to have electricity for a whole day, much less for a whole week or more.

38. The day man fall in love, na that day dey born new mumu.

Translation: The day a man falls in love is the day a new fool is born.

Interpretation: When a man falls deeply in love with a woman, he becomes a fool.

There are countless stories of men doing the unusual when they fall in love with a woman. The song "When a Man Loves a Woman" by Percy Sledge says it all. In the song, it says a man can turn his back on his best friend if his friend tries to put her down. There are cases where a man even turns his back on his own wife and kids when he falls in love with a new woman.

To put it simply, a man in love is a fool. Foolish acts while in love are also applicable to women, but history has tons of records of foolish acts by men. Even in religious texts, there are records of men doing the unthinkable for women. King David became a murderer because of Bathsheba. Samson gave up his most powerful secret because of Delilah. In recent memories, we all know how Clinton almost lost his presidency because of Monica Lewinsky. Some comics said President Clinton was in so much trouble he vowed never to drink whisky again in his life.

39.   You no need spoon or cutlery to chop slap.

Translation: You don't need a spoon or cutlery to eat slap or to receive a slap.

Interpretation: An instrument is not needed to slap someone.

In Nigeria, a child's discipline is taken seriously. When parents want to discipline their kids, they have quite a few tools at their disposal to inflict pain. The common tools used by Nigerian parents for discipline include locally made brooms, belts, *kobokos* (horsewhips), slippers (flip-flops), switch cord, wooden rulers, food paddles, and other available devices at their disposal that can correct indiscipline.

However, parents are quick to use their hands to imprint some digits on a child's face when the child acts out. Slapping someone in the face is quite common in Nigeria; kids are known to get slapped in the face too when they don't follow instructions. The hand is not an improvised tool; hence, you don't need any tool to slap someone in the face.

40. No matter how you take try, you no fit use hand cover pregnancy.

Translation: No matter how hard you try, you cannot use your hand to cover or hide a pregnancy.

Interpretation: You cannot prevent or stop the inevitable.

You cannot stop the rain from falling; neither can you stop the sun from rising.

41. Dem no dey take big prick scare old woman.

Translation: You don't use a big penis to scare an old lady.

Interpretation: You cannot frighten someone who has seen it all.

You can't use the fear of war to threaten a warrior.

42. (a) Woman way never see war, na im dey take hand pack breast when she dey run.

(b) Na when matter never reach matter, na im woman go dey run hold her breast.

Translation (a): A woman who has not experienced war is the one who holds her breasts when she is running.

Translation (b): When there is no major crisis, a woman will be running holding her breast. However, when there is a major crisis, she doesn't hold her breast when she runs.

Interpretation(a): If you have not experienced a major emergency or crisis, you tend to care about trivial things.

Interpretation (b): When there is a major issue, you focus all your attention on dealing with that issue. You disregard every other trivial issue.

(a): When a house is on fire, as a parent, the first things you care about are your kids. You would not be thinking of your clothes or jewellery.

(b): Things that seem important will not be important at all in the face of a major crisis.

43. **Cynthia fit cook! Sandra fit wash! Sophia fit do! Na so King Solomon take marry 700 wives.**

Translation: Cynthia can cook. Sandra knows how to clean. Sophia knows how to make love. That is how King Solomon ended up with 700 wives.

Interpretation: A man who enjoys the pleasure of different women ends up marrying many wives.

In a country where it is OK to marry more than one wife, there is always a justification for marrying more than one woman. Every woman is unique; most times, a man is not content with or satisfied by one woman. There are unique qualities he sees in every woman he meets; the result of women having different unique qualities is that an insatiable man ends up marrying more than one woman.

In Western countries, the men are as guilty as those in Nigeria. American men and those in the Western countries practise polygamy; they just call it a different name. While there is polygamy in Nigeria, the Western countries have sequential polygamy. That is why some of the women in these Western countries have the title ex, as in ex-wife/wives.

44. You don see me finish!

Translation: You have seen all of me.

Interpretation: There is such thing as too much familiarity.

Familiarity breeds contempt. In Nigeria, this statement is quite common when it involves a younger woman and an older man in a relationship. You often see a "big man" (someone seen in high regards) who people respect so much they can't even call him by his first name. However, you will notice a very young girl calling the same big man by his first name without qualms. To really appreciate this explanation, you need to understand how respect towards elders is regarded in Nigerian culture.

45. Head wey no wan think, go carry load.

Translation: The head that is not used to think will be used to carry a load.

Interpretation: If you do not put your brain to good use, you will not be successful.

If you do not go to school to get an education, your opportunity for a better-paying job is limited. This limits you to working menial jobs, which are often hard and pays less.

46. Wen breeze blow, fowl nyash go open.

Translation: When the wind blows, the butt of the chicken will be exposed.

Interpretation: When you are exposed by the truth, people will know your what you are trying to hide.

When you hear Nigerians say, *Breeze don blow oh*, it is like saying, "Breaking news". It's also like saying, "News flash; something has happened." When you hear someone make the statement, just get ready to hear a juicy story.

47. Temper hot, temper hot, e no fit boil yam.

Translation: No matter how hot-tempered you are, the heat of your temper cannot boil a yam.

Interpretation: No matter how angry you get, you still cannot do the impossible.

There is a limitation to your temper. Nigerians have a funny way of telling a person to be cautious when they are terribly angry. This statement is a word of caution; we all have limitations, no matter how hot-tempered we are.

48. Fly wey no dey hear word, na im dey follow dead body enter grave.

Translation: A fly that doesn't listen follows a dead body to the grave.

Interpretation: A person who doesn't listen to good advice ends up in misfortune.

This is often a warning to a person on the verge of self-destruction. In Nigeria, self-destruction is not just about someone involved in hard drugs or other vices. It is often about an inappropriate relationship between a man and a woman. Such relationships draw the attention of friends and families who try to warn of the danger inherent. When the parties involved in an inappropriate relationship don't listen to advice, such statements usually follow.

49. Na man wey no wise, dey slap mosquito wey dey on top im blocos.

Translation: Only a foolish man will swipe at a mosquito on his testicles.

Interpretation: A person who is not smart will often engage himself in a dangerous or life-threatening enterprise.

Nigeria is not alone on this one; all over the world, a man's balls (testicles) are not something to play with. Any activity around that sensitive area must be done with extra caution. When you are dealing with, or involved in a sensitive situation, you will be smart to be extra careful. Only a fool will not be wise enough to handle a very delicate situation with care.

50. Pikin no dey measure blocos with him father.

Translation: A child does not try to compare the size of his testicles with that of his father's.

Interpretation: You do not compare your achievements with the achievements of your parents.

Children are expected to do better than their parents. It makes no sense to raise the issue of your achievement and compare it to that of your parents.

51. Chop this guy money; chop that guy money, na so ashawo take dey start.

Translation: A little spending of Emeka's money, a little spending of Femi's money—that is how prostitution starts.

Interpretation: A lady who loves spending men's money soon ends up being a prostitute.

When you are in a relationship just for the pleasure of spending a man's money while offering to fulfil his desires, you are simply heading into prostitution because you will soon begin to pay back in "kind".

52. Pikin wey no sabi medicine dey call am vegetable.

Translation: A child who doesn't know medicine calls it a vegetable.

Interpretation: A child who cannot distinguish between food and poison will mistake one for the other.

In Nigeria, herbs are used to cure lots of illnesses. One common cure is the cure for malaria. On the other hand, different kinds of herbs are used to make soup, like what every Nigerian calls vegetable soup. While an adult can distinguish which one is for food and which is for medicine, a child often cannot distinguish between the two.

53. E get where u go push goat reach, e go turn bite u.

Translation: There is a threshold where you push a goat, and it will turn around and bite you.

Interpretation: There is a limit to which you can push someone before the person will be forced to react.

An animal like a goat is not an aggressive animal; they see people, and they run away. However, if you chase goats to a point where they are cornered, they will confront you. This also applies to humans; even the meekest person among us will react if pushed beyond a reasonable threshold of endurance.

54. Jollof rice way dey bottom of pot today, go dey on top of cooler tomorrow.

Translation: The rice at the bottom of the pot today will be on top of the food cooler tomorrow.

Interpretation: Your current situation today can change tomorrow.

This is another way for Nigerians to say that no condition is permanent. Just because you are at the bottom of the ladder today doesn't mean you can't be on top tomorrow. If you are facing hardship in life today, you could also live your best life tomorrow. Those who are familiar with Uncle Alagbin (Femi Jarrett) of the *Adio Family* TV show will remember his songs: There is no condition that is permanent in this world! Uncle Alagbin used to do house chores then.

55. I no dey chase woman, I no dey chase woman, after you go complain about prostate cancer.

Translation: I don't chase women, I don't chase women; soon you will complain about prostate cancer.

Interpretation: If you are not sexually active, the probability of having prostate cancer is high.

This is like a warning to those who are celibate. As the saying goes, use it or lose it. If you are not sexually active, you are likely to have prostate cancer. In Nigeria, those who are religious are often against sex before marriage. In a country where people don't get married early because of economic situations, there is a high possibility some will become celibate.

56. That one na only for home video.

Translation: You only see that in the home movies.

Interpretation: That is not the reality.

In movies, especially sci-fi movies, there are lots of visual effects, which, in Nigeria, is called a film trick. There are many scenes that involve impossible actions, things that cannot be achieved in reality. If a man comes and tells his friends he was able to beat up ten men in a fight, most Nigerians will respond by saying *Bros, that na only for home video.*

57. "Ekaete, go and cook for Oga!" Ekaete, go and wash Oga's clothes, na so Oga take marry second wife.

Translation: The housemaid is instructed to prepare food for the man of the house. She is instructed to do the laundry of the man of the house. Soon enough, her status will change from maid to wife.

Interpretation: A woman who allows her maid to take full responsibility of her home is setting the housemaid to be elevated to a second wife by her husband.

There are many stories about men who end up marrying their housemaids in Nigeria. This is usually the fault of the women, according to some people in the society. When a woman asks her maid to do household chores, soon enough, the maid will be doing chores in the bedroom with the man of the house. The maid will be so good at her chore that the man of the house will be forced to promote her to a second wife.

58.   No food for lazy man, no food for lazy man, dat one no concern pikin wey im mama get buka.

Translation: No food for a lazy man, no food for a lazy man, but a person whose mom owns a restaurant is not worried about not having food to eat.

Interpretation: A person who is not ambitious is not worried about the future if his or her family is wealthy.

If your dad is Aliko Dangote or Bill Gates, there are few things you worry yourself about. In other words, if either of these men is your dad, you will not worry about money.

59.   Pikin wey see bald head call am mirror, na him dey chop slap.

Translation: A child who sees the bald head of an elderly person and calls it a mirror gets slapped in the face.

Interpretation: A child who makes a disparaging remark about an elderly person is asking to be spanked.

In Nigeria, you are expected to always show respect to your elders. A child who doesn't know how to address an elder properly will have to be disciplined. The quick and easily accessible tool to discipline a child is the palm of a human hand. No other accessories are needed. Nigeria is the only country I know where they give you a "dirty slap". Every other country just gives you a slap.

60. Who dey purge no dey select toilet!

Translation: Whoever is very pressed to use a toilet doesn't chose a toilet to use.

Interpretation: When you are desperate for something, you choose what is readily available.

As the saying goes, when the desirable is not available, the available becomes the desirable. When you are very hungry, and you have no money to buy food, you will gladly accept what is offered to you. You do not have the luxury of choosing what you would like to eat. Also, when you are very pressed to use a toilet, you do not have the luxury and time to choose the toilet of your choice. In order to prevent a major embarrassing accident, the first available toilet you see is what you use.

61. The man shit inside church.

Translation: The man defecated inside the church.

Interpretation: The man embarrassed himself.

This expression is often used, when someone finds him or herself in a highly embarrassing situation, which is often of his or her own making. An egregious situation in which a person finds him or herself because of his or her careless action will result in Nigerians saying, *You shit inside church*. This is often followed by, *No be ordinary shit; the guy shit water, water shit,* meaning it was a highly embarrassing situation.

62. Custard na just akamu way go Yankee.

Translation: Custard is a local pap that travelled to the United States of America.

Interpretation: There is nothing special about that, or there is nothing special about you. Akamu (pap) and custard are practically the same; akamu is made locally, while custard was engineered to look different.

As humans, we don't realise that we are all the same. Unfortunately, when some people travel to Western countries—often called going abroad in Nigeria—they start acting like they are all that. When Nigerians say this, they are simply saying there is nothing special about you just because you have been to a Western country.

63. Dem don put you inside bottle.

Translation: You have been placed or put inside a bottle.

Interpretation: A spell has been cast on you.

The relationship between a husband and a wife is often scrutinised in Nigeria. Nigerian men are not known to be romantic publicly; and there are things men don't do for their wives publicly just because they don't want to be perceived as being a "woman wrapper". When a man is called a woman wrapper, it means he has been hoodwinked by a woman. When a man shows love to his wife publicly or privately, like by carrying her bag, helping her to cook in the kitchen, or cleaning the house, he is often referred to as a "woman wrapper". You can imagine what is said if a man is found doing his wife's laundry, like washing her panties and underwear. I will leave how some people in Nigeria will react to your imagination.

64. Owerri soup no be poor man soup.

Translation: A good, tasty soup (from Owerri) is not for a poor man.

Interpretation: A beautiful woman is not for a poor man.

The eastern part of Nigeria is known for having varieties when it comes to vegetable soup. Owerri soup is an expensive soup to make; as a result, it is often assumed that a poor person can't afford it. The Owerri soup is a metaphor for a beautiful woman; a beautiful woman is often not associated with poor men.

65. The thing way old man sidon see, even if pikin climb tree, e no go see am.

Translation: What an old person will see just sitting down, a child will climb a tree and still will not be able to see.

Interpretation: Adults are wiser than their kids.

With age comes wisdom; with wisdom, you often have foresight into things that are about to happen. This makes an adult much wiser than a child; adults have been there and done that. This makes an older person seemingly clairvoyant about a situation.

66. I can do without a man. I can do without a man. Na so lesbianism dey take start.

Translation: I don't need any man. I don't need any man. That is the beginning of lesbianism.

Interpretation: When you don't need a man to satisfy you physically, emotionally, and sexually, you are on your way to becoming a lesbian.

These lines might seem like a bashing of independent women. In a society that is very religious like Nigeria, it is expected that a man and a woman are to be together in a relationship. It is also expected that a man provides for the woman and attends to her emotional and sexual needs. When a lady starts saying she doesn't need a man in a society like Nigeria, she will be looked at suspiciously. The first thing that often comes to mind when a woman says she does not need a man is the question of sexual need.

67. I no fit use shame swallow razor blade.

Translation: Shame cannot not make me swallow a razor blade.

Interpretation: An unfortunate or shameful circumstance will not make me do the unthinkable.

Being ashamed should not make you do something ridiculous. Simply put, being ashamed should not make you kill yourself.

68. Over skill na im dey kill monkey.

Translation: Too much skill is what kills the monkey.

Interpretation: When you show off too much when engaged in certain activity, it will lead to your demise.

This is actually a word of caution for people who try to impress others. When a fighter is in the ring and suddenly gains advantage over his opponent, instead of finishing his opponent he decides to act silly (showboat). Such actions often come around to bite the fighter who had an upper hand earlier.

69. Dem no dey find virgin for maternity ward.

Translation: They don't find a virgin in the maternity ward.

Interpretation: You have no business being where you are.

This is used to refer to being in an impossible position. It is about knowing your place in life, knowing your role at a job, and knowing your position in life. We don't expect a truck driver to be in the cockpit of a plane. This is what Nigerians will say to you if you are not in the right place or position.

70. Pikin wey go strong go strong, no be till dem name am Samson.

Translation: A child who will be strong will be strong; he doesn't have to be named Samson.

Interpretation: A person will achieve what he or she will achieve in life; it's not dictated by what the person is called or the name he or she is given. Que sera sera.

You cannot make your child a good boxer by calling him Muhammed Ali. You cannot make a kid a good kung fu fighter by calling the kid Bruce Lee.

71. **Dem no dey ask a married woman where she get belle from.**

Translation: You don't ask a married woman who got her pregnant.

Interpretation: When things are obvious, you don't ask questions.

It is one thing to ask a single lady who got her pregnant. It is a different ballgame entirely when you ask a married woman who got her pregnant. Who else is supposed to get a married woman pregnant, especially if the husband is alive? However, we all know there are exceptional cases.

72. **Pikin wey like party rice no supposed to fear dance.**

Translation: A child who loves the food served at a party is not supposed to be afraid to dance at the party.

Interpretation: If you love women, you should not be afraid to spend heavily. If you love to fight, you should not be afraid of blood.

Certain things go hand in hand; if you don't like to work, you should not be afraid of being broke.

73. **Na when soldier slap you, you go sabi say police na your friend**.

Translation: When a soldier slaps you, that's when you will remember the police is your friend.

Interpretation: One bad situation often makes you realise an earlier situation you thought was bad was not that bad after all.

When those close to you disappoint you, that is when you will remember those who are not too close to you.

74. Weytin concern vultures with barber?

Translation: What business does a vulture have with a barber?

Interpretation: How is that my business?

This saying is just like the saying in number four. This is what Nigerians will often say when things that are none of their concern are brought to their attention.

75. Person wey naked no dey chook hand for pocket.

Translation: A person who is stark naked has no pocket to put his or her hand in.

Interpretation: If you do not have a car, you don't get a driver's license. You don't engage in conversation when you don't have an idea of the topic being discussed or have any opinion to offer.

You cannot give what you do not have.

76. Today's newspaper na tomorrow's Suya wrap.

Translation: Today's newspaper will be used to wrap grilled beef or barbeque tomorrow.

Interpretation: While you are held at high esteem today, tomorrow you may not be regarded or recognised.

This is also a way of saying no condition is permanent. You are held at high esteem because of the value and influence of your position today. However, tomorrow you could lose that position suddenly, and nobody will value you anymore.

This is quite common with people who hold government position; they are like superstars when they are ministers in government. Once the person is out of power, as they say in Nigeria, *Nobody go look your face*, meaning no one will care to visit you or even say hello to you.

77. **Who read am naim serious, who pass naim know book.**

Translation: The person who reads is serious; the person who passes is the smart one.

Interpretation: It is all about the result and not the effort.

While your effort will be commended, it is your result that is really valued.

78. **No matter how lizard do press-up reach, e no fit get chest like alligator.**

Translation: No matter the amount of push-up exercises the lizard does, it can never have a chest like an alligator.

Interpretation: No matter how hard you try to imitate someone or be someone else, you can never be that person. In other words, you can only be you, no matter how you try to be someone else.

In Nigeria, when someone is engaged in a fruitless activity or embarking on a fruitless journey, such a statement is often made. When you are trying to achieve what is not achievable, you will often hear such statements as well.

79. Stone wey you see dey fall from up, no suppose hit you.

Translation: A stone you see falling from the sky is not supposed to hit you.

Interpretation: Whatever you are anticipating should not come as a surprise.

This is similar to number twenty-three. A fraudster you know should not be able to defraud you.

80. Who dash monkey banana?

Translation: Who gave a monkey a gift of banana?

Interpretation: This is a rhetorical question when someone is trying to convey a message of a wishful desire that could not be achieved at the moment.

This is like the expression of, "I wish." When Nigerians are engaged in a conversation and someone teases another person by saying, "You should be in the Bahamas enjoying yourself, or somewhere you desire," the reply in most Western countries for such statement would be, "I wish." In Nigeria, the response would be, *Who dash monkey banana?*

81. Person way bend down dey look somebody yansh, na so another person they look him own yansh too.

Translation: When you bend down to look at someone's behind, someone else will also be looking at yours.

Interpretation: When you get involved in other people's business, people will get in your own business too.

To put it simply, what goes around comes around.

82. **When goat dey laugh after e hear say lion dey around, person need to know the kind grass wey the goat dey chop.**

Translation: When a goat is still laughing when it hears a lion is around, there is a need to check what kind of grass the goat is eating.

Interpretation: When a person is aware of a pending danger and starts laughing, there is a need to examine that person or have him or her evaluated.

If you are in your parlour (living room) and fire breaks out suddenly in your kitchen and you are still seated calmly and smiling, it is obvious you need a serious evaluation or psychiatric evaluation.

83. **I go marry you. I go marry you. Na so dem chop Amaka (Fiona) seven times.**

Translation: I will marry you; I will marry you! That is how they slept with Amaka (Fiona) seven times.

Interpretation: The promise of marriage in a relationship has led to women being taken advantage of by men.

In a country where getting married is becoming more difficult because of the tough economic situation, a young lady is easily swayed by the promise of a man who says he wants to settle down with her in marriage. Soon enough, the man changes his mind

99

after he has tasted the cookie (if you know what I mean). All talk about settling down is out the window, and the young lady is left heartbroken. In due time, the lady recovers and soon falls in love again. She faces another disappointment. Before you know it, she has dated many guys who promise her marriage.

84. Na person wey never see problem dey use good English dey pray.

Translation: A person who has not seen a major problem uses the Queen's English to pray.

Interpretation: When you have faced a major problem, you pray in a language you are most comfortable with, or you use native dialect to pray.

It is well documented that there are many native languages spoken in Nigeria; however, the lingua franca is English. Since Nigeria was colonised by Great Britain, it is expected that Nigerians are good at speaking the Queen's English. Nigerians are more comfortable speaking Nigerian Pidgin English and much more so when they speak with their native dialect. So, it is expected, when you are in a desperate need and you need help from the Almighty, you will make your request in a language you are most comfortable with.

85. Na only time e go take, stammerer go pronounce him papa name.

Translation: In due time, a person who stutters will eventually pronounce his or her father's name.

Interpretation: It is just a matter of time; you will always get to your destination.

People who stutter sometimes find it difficult to get their words out; despite the challenge, they eventually get their statements across. In Nigeria, this is a way of saying that, if you are patient, you will achieve your objective.

86. Person wey dey sell coffins for market, no dey call out customers to buy him goods.

Translation: A person who sells caskets does not place an ad for people to buy their casket.

Interpretation: You don't need an ad for goods that are necessary or essential.

When was the last time you saw an ad for salt on any medium of communication?

87. No drink Panadol for another person headache.

Translation: Don't take a medication for someone else's ailment.

Interpretation: Do not let the plight of others become your burden.

This is another way Nigerians will tell you to mind your business, and don't let other people's plights give you a headache.

88. The fresh leaf wey laugh dry leaf wey fall down, forget say one day em' self too go dry and fall down.

Translation: A fresh leaf on a tree that laughs at a dry fallen leaf has forgotten that, someday, it will also become dry and fallen leaf.

Interpretation: If you laugh or make fun of an older person, remember you will grow old yourself.

If you laugh at people's mistakes, remember, in due time you will make mistakes too.

89. Crayfish waka.

Translation: Crayfish walk.

Interpretation: You're on a fruitless errand.

When Nigerian embark on a trip or a journey to find something or to pay someone a visit and the whole purpose of the journey is not achieved, you will hear a Nigerian say, *Na Crayfish waka*.

90. Person wey borrow shoes go party, no dey dance anyhow.

Translation: When you borrow shoes to go to a party, you are more careful how you dance.

Interpretation: You are more careful when you use another person's property.

This statement is just a piece of advice on how to treat stuff you borrow from people. Handle with care what you borrow from other people.

91. Man no fit get brother on top mango tree, make e dey chop unripe mango.

Translation: You can't have a brother own a mango tree and be eating an unripe or bad mango.

Interpretation: You cannot have someone in a place of power or influence and not benefit from that person's influence.

For things to go your way or for you to get what you want is all about having connections. You cannot have someone close to you high up in an establishment and not be benefiting from that person's position.

92. Na rain wey fall, make dog and goat dey the same place.

Translation: The rain is the reason you will find a dog and a goat in the same place.

Interpretation: Certain situations will put you in a place with people you have no business being with.

Circumstances will force you to be in the same place with people you have no business associating with or people you do not want to associate with. A simple example is you being in the same gas station with the person who stole your lover from you. When you run out of gas in your car, you are forced to find the nearest gas station you see. Even if your most hated enemy is in that gas station, you have no option but to stop and get gas for your car.

93. Na how man for do, na im make man join Nigerian Police.

Translation: The lack of job options is the reason a person will join the Nigerian Police Force.

Interpretation: When the best is not available, the available becomes the best option.

The job of a police officer in Nigeria is not a very enticing job; the police in Nigeria are known to not be paid well. The people who join the police always join because quality jobs are not available.

When you are out of options, the only available option becomes your best hope.

Imagine writing the Joint Admission Matriculation Board (JAMB) exam—most often, students in Nigeria will choose the premier or prestigious universities as their first choice. Some first-choice universities are University of Ibadan (UI), Ahmadu Bello University (ABU), University of Ife (now Obafemi Awolowo University), University of Lagos (UNILAG), University of Nigeria (Nsukka), and Yaba College of Technology. However, *when go no go* (when things do not work out), you settle for the next available university or college. Furthermore, if university opportunities are not forthcoming, you find the best polytechnic. Even at that level, Yaba Tech will come first.

94. Chop and clean mouth.

Translation: Eat and clean your mouth.

Interpretation: Keep it on the down low.

When you clean your mouth after eating, it is because you do not want to leave evidence of what you ate. You simply do not want to tell the world you just finished eating. In Nigeria, this statement applies when you deliberately do something, and you go out of your way not to let anyone know—just like having an illicit affair.

95. Na yam?

Translation: Is it yam? (a rhetorical question)

Interpretation: Is it easy? (a rhetorical question)

In Nigeria, there is a folk story about the agama lizard. The lizard is said to have fallen from a tall palm tree and landed on its chest. The lizard is quick to praise itself after landing on its chest, saying, "If you don't praise me, I will praise myself. If you think it is easy, why don't you jump from a palm tree and land on your chest?"

When you hear Nigerians ask this question, they are not expecting an answer from you because the right answer is quite obvious. When someone does something spectacular or achieves something great or attains a college or university degree, such a statement may be made.

96. Wetin concern blind man with NEPA?

Translation: What business does a blind man have with an electric power company?

Interpretation: How is that my business?

In Nigeria, NEPA stands for National Electric Power Authority and is the body responsible for providing electric power to the entire nation. The funny question here is, What business does a blind person have with the power company that provides light?

97. Monkey born one pikin, two die.

Translation: Monkey gave birth to one baby, and two babies died.

Interpretation: You're making unnecessary excuses or making a statement that's not relevant to the issue at hand.

Let's say you owe someone money; you set a date for when you're going to pay, but when that time comes, you start talking about why you cannot pay. The statement will be relevant; it describes the excuse no one wants to hear. You will often hear Nigerians say: *You promise me say na today you go pay me, after how many months. I come here now as you tell me to come. Now you dey tell story of how monkey born one, two die.*

98. Person wey owe landlord house rent, no dey pound yam for compound.

Translation: A tenant who owes the landlord rent does not pound yam in the compound.

Interpretation: A person who has an outstanding debt to settle does not show or display wealth.

You should be cautious when it comes to how you operate or handle yourself in the presence of your creditors.

99. I resemble mugu for your eyes?

Translation: Do I look like a mugu in your eyes?

Interpretation: Do I look like a fool to you?

Nigerians often ask this question when they figure out you're trying to outsmart them.

100. Leave story for tortoise.

Translation: Leave the story for the tortoise.

Interpretation: Just let it go.

When Nigerians are tired of an explanation or are tired of talking about a topic for a prolonged period, you will often hear them make such a statement. Sometimes, you might have useful information to offer; when that information is not useful at that moment, don't be surprised when you hear a Nigerian say, *Leave story for tortoise!*

CONCLUSION

The best is still yet to come out of Nigeria. There is still more creativity to give to the world. Despite enormous challenges facing Nigerians, Nigerians are surviving. The worst kind of pain is suffering amid plenty; Nigerians are indeed suffering amid plenty. There are two types of changes needed in Nigeria—economic change and social change. Economic change usually takes longer while social change can happen quickly. One social change Nigerians can implement immediately is saying no to the use of horsewhips on Nigerians by any law enforcement officer. Nigerians are not animals. If Nigerians are not respected by their own government, other countries will not respect Nigeria and Nigerians. Every human being should be treated with dignity, and Nigerians are not exempt. The culture of people throwing trash on the street can be changed without the use of the entire campaign of WAI (War Against Indiscipline). However, there are some positive things that can be borrowed from the WAI campaigns and implemented without law enforcement treating people like lower animals.

Communication should be sent to all Nigerian embassies all over the world on how to attend to the needs of every Nigerian. Charity, they say, begins at home; if every Nigerian is treated with dignity, then all Nigerians will have a sense of belonging. If a country does not show love and respect for its citizens through its laws, why would those citizens show love for that country? More so, why would any other country respect and treat you better? People in power are often quick to quote John Fitzgerald Kennedy (the thirty-fifth president of the United States): "Ask not what your country can do for you, but what you can do for your country." That could be said by the American president because his country had provided social security for its citizens, good roads, security, and a democracy that every American believed in back then. What has the Nigerian government provided for its people? The Nigerian leader has no moral right to ask the question JKF asked his fellow citizens.

Policing is about community relationship, but it seems that the mere fact that it is called Nigerian Police Force means there must be excessive force. There is a need to train police in Nigeria to see civilians as people they swore an oath to protect and not to brutalise or oppress. There is a need to improve police intelligence with regards to policing in Nigeria. There is a need for innovation and improvement when it comes to the strategies for solving major crimes in Nigeria. Countless great minds have been murdered without a chance of finding the murderers. If the minister of justice (Chief Bola Ige) could not get justice, what is the hope for the average Nigerian? Nigeria used to have what was known as CID (Criminal Investigation Division). What happened to that division? There is no standard existence of a forensic division in the Nigerian Police Force. How can crimes be solved?

It is easy to pass a law saying law enforcement officers have no right to hit or put their hands on any Nigerian, except if they must protect themselves from attack. It is funny how law enforcement officers will hit Nigerians, and when the people fight back, the officers will accuse the person, saying, "Who dares to fight back and disrespect the police uniform?" If law enforcement officers in Nigeria knew their oath of office, they would understand that they themselves are the ones disrespecting their uniform. Hopefully, Nigerian police will be an example to the world. People are tired of Nigerians using Western countries as a standard. Let Nigerians, for once, set the standard for the rest of the world.

Nigeria does not realise the security implications of a sitting president travelling overseas for medical treatment! What does it say about the healthcare system in Nigeria?

Finally, the size of government must be reduced. We need to decentralise the government in Nigeria. Nigerians are not asking for too much. Just give them constant electricity, good roads, and potable drinking water; and you'll see every other thing fall in place. There is still a lot of creativity yet to be seen from Nigeria and Nigerians.

The creation of the Nigerian Pidgin English (or simply Pidgin) by Nigerians is genius. All that Nigerians have going for them is the ability to use the language spoken to survive the daily hustle in a land that is supposed to be flowing with milk and honey. Besides this, they must survive the daily tears, pains, and sorrows.

I yartar! (I'm more than tired! The next level after being tired)
E don finish. (The end.)

ABOUT THE AUTHOR

Mustapha Anako
The Nigerian Host

Photograph by Rachael Ometere Anako

I am currently an instructor at Miami Arts Charter in Miami, Florida. I lived and worked in Nigeria before migrating to the United States of America in January 2005 to join my wife (Ahuoiza Nene Anako). We are blessed with two children (Marc Inda-Enesi and Rachael Ize-Ometere).

Before migrating to the United States, I worked with an organisation known as Towncriers (a subsidiary of Bates Cosse)—a marketing agency. Due to my job as a sales promoter and a project supervisor, I was fortunate to have travelled intensively around Nigeria, supervising various events involving product launches, game shows, and various concerts, each requiring street promotions.

My love for being the host at weddings, wedding anniversaries, and naming ceremonies (this is a customary ceremony within the Nigerian community) has ultimately led me to write my first book, which you now have in your hands.

I truly hope you enjoy this unconventional book.

Printed in the United States
by Baker & Taylor Publisher Services